Step into My World

Step into My World

A Collection of Poems

Dave Navsa

DB

DIADEM BOOKS

Step into My World: A Collection of Poems

Published by Diadem Books
Distribution coordination by Spiderwize

For information, please contact:

Diadem Books
16 Lethen View
Tullibody
Alloa
FK10 2GE UK

www.diadembooks.com

ISBN: 978-1-908026-15-6

Dedication

Always in our hearts, always on our minds
In Loving memory of our father
Gone but never forgotten
We love and miss you very much.

This book is dedicated to our

Gemma and Tara

"The power of the Pen is infinitively superior to the Bomb or Bullet."

Table of Contents

Acknowledgements

This book is published with the kind permission of the Author's family—
his Mother, Dorothy, Sister Rose and Daughters Gemma and Tara.

Special thanks are due to the Reverend Father Doug Snoswell who has been of tremendous help to me in the development and promotion of this collection of poems.

Cover Picture from a Mural, ‘Poet's thoughts’.

Cover reproduced by kind permission of:

Denise and Terry, proprietors of Tiny Tim’s Teashop, Rochester

Jamie Montgomery, Commission Artist

Ray Banks, Photographer

Foreword

This book is a collection of Poems, in memory of, and in tribute to, our close friend Dave who was tragically and prematurely taken from us on 1st January 2011. The Book is comprised of his original manuscripts found in his effects and published with the kind permission of his next of kin. It is an appropriate and fitting sequel to his first book *Climb Aboard My Bus: Pictures in Verse* published in 2007.

Dave was a charismatic and complex character. He was modest, reticent and sometimes introspective, but he had an excellent and often mischievous sense of humour capable of captivating a room full of people with mirth. Just as an artist blends his colours to create a canvas, Dave had an innate talent to weave rich tapestries of words to describe events, people and places, whether minute or momentous. He could paint pictures in words, not only accurately depicting the scenes, but also reflecting his mood whilst writing.

He first visited the historic, former city of Rochester, featured in the Dickens' novel *Great Expectations* on a school trip at the age of 9 and fell in love with the place. In 2005 he came to live in Rochester, made many friends, some of whom helped with this Book. He spent much time in the High Street and in the grounds of the Cathedral and castle. He found the surroundings therapeutic and inspirational. Dave often observed artists painting local scenes and would later create his own pictures in verse.

In the lead Poem, 'Rochester High Street', he manages in a snapshot, as if through a camera lens, to encapsulate the history, activities and even the atmosphere of the place. 'Anyone for Tennis' evokes memories of stirring battles at Jacksons Field courts—far removed from Centre Court, but the contest to return service no less enthusiastic or intense. The Poem 'Will you?' reveals a deeply sentimental person. The Poem is almost subliminal communication with words that would, in reality, be impossible to say to someone close.

The panoramic view from the Castle ramparts, the immaculate grounds, the Cannon and steps leading to the neat flowerbeds, is now Dave's spiritual home overlooking the Esplanade and the River Medway.

The process of collating these poems has touched all our emotions. We hope that when you read them you will "Step into his World" and share with us some of the joy of knowing him.

Sandra and Maurice

Preface

As in his previous collection of poems, *Climb Aboard My Bus*, this collection, *Step Into My World,* is a poetic and psychological *tour de force*, a guided tour through the poet's imaginative mind. It is a potpourri of vivid pictures, moods and emotions. As before, the poems are gems that sparkle with pleasing rhyme and vivid life! They constitute, as it were, a photographic album, or to vary the metaphor, a necklace of different gems, presenting different facets that sparkle in different ways, depending on the light that captures them.

So many of the poems take the form of a journey, or an invitation to join the poet on a journey of discovery—hence the titles suggesting travel like 'Climb Aboard My Bus', 'Step Into My Mind', 'Walk Inside My Brain', 'In My World', 'The Train', and 'Runaway Train'. The poems can be delightfully light-hearted, sparking with humour, but there are those that resonate on a deeper level, venturing into the darker side of the human psyche where we are aware of a world in need of peace, a world in conflict, unable to communicate, having lost the simple ability of joined-up thinking, unable to see the simplicity of love and beauty. 'Night Walker' and 'Slogan', for example, reflect an abiding theme – the dichotomy of the rich and the poor – where the poet identifies sympathetically with the poor who are trampled upon and ignored by 'men in suits'. Often the protagonist is a ghostly presence (in 'Ghost'), the omniscient observer, or traveller, drifting, objective, recording, holding up a dispassionate mirror to the unfeeling reality of our times. The loneliness not only of the neglected, the forgotten, but of the poet himself, often make the journey a poignant experience. Appropriately, perhaps, the collection ends with 'An Earthquake Happened', written long before the earthquake and tsunami in Japan, which brings vividly to mind the awful suffering of the people who experience the devastation of such disasters.

David Navsa is a wordsmith who is inspired by life and its effect on people and events, whether spiritual or emotional; love, insanity, fantasy, and a wide variety of subjects are captured in a veritable play on words. An imaginative and versatile poet, he can write on demand on virtually any subject!

—Charles Muller, Diadem Books

Snapshot of Rochester Cathedral taken by the Author
from the arrowloops (windows) of Rochester Castle.

ROCHESTER HIGH STREET

The High Street blends
Like the colours of the rainbow
From multi-coloured costumes
To artificial snow
History stands tall
Below the musicians that play
Dickens still roams the street
Mingling with the ghosts of today
The tourists roll in
A modern invading force
To capture the castle on film
And follow the river's course
The silent artist roams
With a canvass that speaks
The multi-lingual barter and browse
Amongst the rare books and antiques
Centuries of solid stonework
From a bygone Norman age
Plays host each and every year
To modern acts upon a stage
There's an arch-way to the past
That still seems to blend
There are watering holes and tea-houses
Where you can still find a friend
What used to be a silent vault
Is now a trendy sound
Long forgotten Roman roads
Still exist below the ground
There's a shop that leans
Where photographers seem to meet
It's a place where ancient and modern
Walk hand and hand along the street.

STEP INTO MY MIND

Step into my mind
And make sure you have a grip
No psychedelic glasses
Can prepare you for this trip

Leave all inhibitions
And the need to analyse
For this is where honesty
Lives with no disguise

There are no undertones
On polished illusions
Just a world laid bare
Of all its delusions

Walk with me uninhibited
Through no man's land
Watch the past, present and future
Disappear like sand

There are no fake eyes
To lead you astray
Only cold stark reality
To pave your way

There are no fools here
To disrupt your soul
No trusted minds
Longing for control

No new boss with an upgraded room
To tell you that change comes with a new broom

WALK INSIDE MY BRAIN

Come and walk inside my brain
When I'm feeling slightly insane
If you have enough love
You can buy yourself a ticket
On a pink imaginary train.

Watch the sun as it roses at night
Climb inside Pandora's box
Join the school of cunning
And become a regular fox.

If you're feeling a little small
Come and have yourself a ball
If you have enough love
You can buy Humpty Dumpty
And even knock down his wall.

Watch the invisible people
All lining up for a fix
A boiling pot of answers
A psychedelic cultural mix.

Come and climb up my tree
And see the meaning of insanity
If you have enough love
You can buy back your dreams
And turn them into reality.

Watch the end of the beginning
Through the eyes of a lost child
Then paint all of your visions
And let them run totally wild.

IN MY WORLD

I lose myself in my writing
That's when I'm at my happiest…
When I lose myself
When I no longer have to think
Of who I am or what I am
The extra bonus is…
When I have to think of nobody
I can lose myself
In a fantasy world
A world to which
I really belong
And feel most comfortable
I say this as no disrespect
To anyone
It's a difficult burden to bear
To be an exception.

Breathing space is when
You're surrounded by Oxygen
And fresh thoughts
Isolation is when
You're surrounded by Carbon Monoxide
And stale thoughts
Learning to balance the two
Is an art.

Do not focus on
The individual
And lose sight
Of the intent.

Do not focus on
The intent
And lose sight
Of the individual…

CLIMB ABOARD MY BUS

Climb aboard my bus
If you're feeling low
With nowhere to go
And nothing to do
Relax and let go
And feel the flow
Of just being you.

Climb aboard my bus
If you're feeling confused
With a heart that's bruised
And losing its pace
Float down stream
In your own dream
And in your own space.

Climb aboard my bus
If you're feeling down
With a matching frown
And a mood that's blue
Everything is granted
And nothing is implanted
All you see is all that's true

Climb aboard my bus
If you have to think twice
And everything is a price
You have to pay
We're all the same
Though a different name
The same characters, the same play.

GHOST

I walk the night
Just like a ghost
It's my party
And I am the host.

A chilly wind blows
As my guests arrive
They have see-through clothes
But they survive.

I float on high
Just like a ghost
It's my party
And I raise a toast.

An eerie silence reigns
As my guests all smile
There are no rattling chains
As in they file.

I slip through the walls
Just like a ghost
It's my party
And I am free to boast.

They came from afar
And slip into place
They don't need a car
Just a space.

I am earth bound
Just like a ghost
It's my party
And I make the most.

NIGHT WALKER

A bag lady fills her bags surrounded by stench
Her aching bones long for the comfort of a bench
The neon lights shimmer with the shaking of the clubs
And the spirited gatherings have begun in the pubs
Boats on the river are partying until dawn
As someone passes by with a casual yawn
A galloping dog cuts the air as if in panic
And the faces on the late train are somewhat manic
A candle on a restaurant table is glowing
Latin American disco music is flowing
From wall to wall a rubber-legged drunk stumbles
His hand in his pocket hopelessly fumbles
Drawn to the aromas of Indian curries
A rat caught in the light hurriedly scurries
A half naked girl is drawing her curtain
Her true intentions are not very certain
The lonely walk by without any friends
Kicking the chips and the cigarette ends
The girls of the night stomp by in their boots
And the begging tramp holds on to his roots
The dubious men with the eyes of a cat
Makes you wonder exactly where they're at
Alcohol takes the place of blood in the veins
Relaxing all the day's stresses and strains
Friday night rises just like the dead
Time is non-existent before the Monday morning dread
Suddenly the shining moon and distant star
Becomes very close and not that far
I'm one of the silent, a non-talker
I'm one of the ghosts, a night walker.

SOMEWHERE ELSE

I'd rather be somewhere else
Than where I am
Instead of caviar
I'd rather have eggs and ham
Sometimes I'd rather not
Be the decider
Instead of champagne
I'd rather have cider
Instead of a peck on the cheek
I'd rather a kiss on the lips
But sometimes it's really nice
To have burger and chips
There's nothing like the twinkle
In a sexy girl's eyes
But it really can't compare
To steak and kidney pies
Miles of sunset views
And piles of ready cash
Could never really compare
To a plate of sausage and mash
The warm summer sun
And gentle sea breeze
Will always come second
To an omelette with cheese

TIME MARCHES ON

Time marches on
But the good times will stay
Think of the good times
And the bad will go away

Watch the river
How it bends and twists
Become like the river
Even in the mists

When lightning and thunder
Begin to tear you apart
Listen to the peace
That rains in your heart

And when you're caught out
On that runaway train
Think of all those suffering
In poverty and pain

Time may march on
But we're all just the same
We're all manic chess pieces
In a manic chess game

TAKE A TRIP

Come take a trip
And visit with me
A land of corkscrews
And insanity
Where what goes up
Cannot come down
Where the land of gravity
Is the other way round

See scarlet streaks in the sun
Giant zips that come undone
What could lead to better things
Than giant frogs in giant swamps?

[Unfinished poem]

WHO ARE YOU?

Who are you when you are not you?
Are you someone just passing through?
Are you someone in someone else's imagination
Or perhaps an idea in someone else's creation?

Who are you, what are you and where
Are you then, now or even here?
Are you the urge that you cannot resist
Or perhaps in reality you do not exist?

You are what you are but what you are
Are you false, lost or even true?
Are you that spark that ignites your life
Or just a figment of your very own strife?

PEOPLE

People don't talk, they scream
People don't live, they dream
People don't walk, they stumble
People done write, they crumble

Lost in a world of make believe
Never giving but happy to receive
Always running but getting nowhere
Forever listening but they cannot hear

Like a train on only one track
They look forward by looking back
Always stirring with only one aim
That life in total is but a game

Full of hatred and full of spite
Every wrong has to be a right
Eyes open but the mind is blind
Searching in the dark but cannot find

CIVILISATION

Civilisation is a creation in the art form
It is the movement on the shoulders of a storm
Constantly drifting in and out of sleeps
It shines when it smiles, it rains when it weeps

Civilisation is a novelty taken for granted
It's a barren land where seeds are planted
Like a lifetime of new dawns in the making
It's a cauldron of ideas for the taking

Civilisation is a furnace of devils and preachers
Crammed with knowledge but without any teachers
Locked in chains and bound together
Moving from present to the future forever

Civilisation is the right key to the wrong door
It's the foundation that builds an invisible floor
Always seeking but unable to find
That most precious desire, a total peace of mind

I AM TWO

I am two people with only two eyes
I am two characters within one disguise
I am two speakers with only one voice
I have many possibilities but only one choice

I am two thinkers with only one brain
I have many tracks but only one train
I am two actors with only one part
I have many emotions but only one heart

I am two people with only one link
A chain of thoughts unable to think
I am two souls locked in one cell
Two prisoners forever in one hell

LIE DOWN

From January to December
Lie down and surrender
Hold up the white flag
Hold your tongue and do not brag
Any combined thought is strictly your own
Lie down, surrender to your throne
Disregard the feeling to pursue
These feelings are only given to a few
Time is tight like trousers round the waist
And the bitterness is the only flavour you'll taste
Lie down and give nothing to the void
Or your aching soul will always be annoyed
Lie down and give in to the sound of the drum
Let your mind drift and your body become numb
When your eye becomes your worst spy
Lie down and let the world go
If I make you feel like I do
Then all you face cannot be true
And when the sun sets on another confused day
Lie down and let your soul slip away
If all you think of becomes a drag
Lie down, stretch out, hold up the flag

COMMUNICATION

Across the air waves from land to land
Across the sea from nation to nation
People are walking hand in hand
With a certain lack of communication

Behind dark windows
Classified innuendos
Are written everyday
But no one will say
A lack of communication

Across all cultures from land to land
Across platforms from station to station
People are walking hand in land
With a total lack of communication

Behind metal gates
Classified mistakes
Are stored away
But no one dares to say
A lack of communication

Across all religions from land to land
Across destruction from degradation to degradation
People are walking hand in hand
With a complete lack of communication

Behind closed eyes
Classified lies
Are on the agenda
But no one will surrender
To the lack of communication

MAKE SURE

If every joke has to be lewd
And you won't listen to anyone who's older
When every bottle must be unscrewed
Make sure your head is on your shoulder

If you're a shark with a card up your sleeve
And every word you speak is just a lie
When the path before you leads you to deceive
Make sure you hold your hands up high

If the fever in your head makes your blood boil
And brute force becomes more than a smack
When the brain in your head tightens like a coil
Make sure you don't look back

If your actions justify your morality
And the thoughts in your head make you swear
When your dreams all emerge as reality
Make sure you don't sink into despair

POETIC

I'm a poetic tailor
I'm a pied piper with his flute
Give me your ideas
And I'll make you a suit

I'm a poetic sailor
I'm an avid mountaineer
Give me your request
And I'll bring you back a souvenir

I'm a poetic diver
I'm constantly looking for pleasure
Give me your wishes
And I'll bring you back a treasure

I'm a poetic spaceman
I'm a traveller of speed
Give me your vision
And I'll find you what you need

I'm a poetic philosopher
I'm a maker of schemes
Give me your soul
And I'll give you my dreams

GRANDMA

From youth throughout the ages
A life full of many stages
A book stacked with pages
From grandma with love

From happiness to despairs
From many a struggle and many fears
A book filled with love and cares
From grandma with love

From a time of many loose ends
And the passing of many friends
A book of memories and trends
From grandma with love

From an age that passes by
From many a low to many a high
A book of smiles to make you cry
From grandma with love

BIBLICAL THOUGHTS

Jesus spread his words
And asked people to trust
He said to Simon Peter
Go and do what you must

Whether paved or rocky
You must follow the track
And when you reach the end
There's no turning back

Moses took his tablets
And with his staff by his side
He preached his commandments
And left people to decide

Whatever your feelings
Your fate has begun
Whatever you think, whatever you do
Has already been done

Cain became centre stage
With a vision in each eye
Only he could decide
Whether Abel should die

Whatever you plan
Is your very own choice
And the decision you make
Is your very own voice

INCOMPLETE

I once had a cat
He went out one day
And never came back
Leaving me incomplete

Everything comes to those who wait
Or so they say
But sometimes tomorrow is just too late

I once had friends
Then they went away
And never came back
Leaving me incomplete

Everything has a meaning and reason
Or so they say
But sometimes fate feels like treason

I once had visions
Which melted away
And never came back
Leaving me incomplete

Everything is and as it should be
Or so they say
But sometimes to be incomplete is not to be free

BOXES

A sudden urgency of sadness
Fills the boxes in my head
The thin line between sanity and madness
Becomes a surge of dread

An outstretched hand
Is not a command
Or a gesture to demand
Just a way to understand

A sudden surge of not knowing
Fills the boxes in my head
The once dead roots are now growing
Becoming solid like lead

When you don't want to think
And you don't want to blink
When you don't want to drink
It's no reason for being extinct

A sudden fear of the unknown
Fills the boxes in my head
The once logical structure is now thrown
And becomes confusion instead

WATCH THE RIVER

If you believe in the game of lies
And social contact is just a game
If the sand is reflected through the eyes
And that who you are is just a name
Then watch the river as it flows

If you believe in sitting in the dark
And mixing with people is just a joke
If life is created by just a spark
And that your confusion is only smoke
Then watch the river as it flows

If you believe you are what you wear
And if people seem a part of you
If eternity feels like it's very near
And that you have so much left to do
Then watch the river as it flows

If you believe happiness is something you find
And social drop-outs are part of you
If the feeling of love is constantly blind
And that coming last is nothing new
Then watch the river as it flows

WELCOME TO MY WORLD

Welcome to my world
My little alien friend
Where the straight and narrow
Is completely round the bend
Where life consists of mental press-ups
Framed Disney donkeys
And days of continuous mess-ups
I'll show you how isolation
Can keep you from being sane
How the joys of childhood
Is expressed in pain
How it takes years of practice
Listening to the dumb
Whilst banging your head
Until your brain is numb
I'll take you to a world
That thrives on cold fear
Deep into my mind
And the depths of despair
It's not for the squeamish
Or those who are afraid
It's a prison for the souls
That have debts unpaid
I'll show you how the thoughts of suicide
Could really be a lot of fun
Where you can never ever get away
No matter how far you run
I'm now a part of a cosmic plan
That keeps me drifting in space
But you see, like you, I'm alienated
Now part of a different race
Welcome to my world
To my Jekyll and Hyde wonderland
Where I'm free to roam in black and white
A surrealism that no one can understand

RELIGIOUS THOUGHTS

Are there two-faced churches,
Nuns who whip with birches?
Is there one good book on the shelf
For laying the dead by yourself?
Is there a holy shrine
With no glass of wine?
Is man counted by the collars he wears,
Is his soul measured by the cross he bears?
Will he who walks alone
Be the first to cast the stone?
Will monks in their frocks
Be in for some shocks,
And will the shipwrecked few
Be only Satan and his crew?
Unless I swallow religion
Am I part of a division?
Will all that's holy and divine
Be one day yours and not mine?
Is there a special place I will go
Because the bible tells me so?

CLOSE TO HOME

I sit outside a Coffee Bar
Close to home but very far
Trying hard to forget
Trying to suppress regret

I watch couples holding hands
I think how lucky they are
Close to home but very far

I sip my coffee, smoke my cigarette
I review my mental debt
I follow the music from a car
Close to home but very far

I watch people living their lives
As the mist rises from the far
Close to home but very far

Another minute goes by, another car
Close to home but very far
Another cigarette kills the doubt
As father time begins to shroud

AT WHAT COST?

The prophets say...
Things get better in the long run
Dark clouds are replaced by the sun
Let your thoughts consist of all that's nice
But at what cost is the sacrifice?

Experience is like an ageing wine
The longer it takes, the more refine
If you do it once, you can do it twice
But at what cost is the sacrifice?

The angels say...
That God is within all of us
And that there is no need to fuss
The variety of life is but a spice
But at what cost is the sacrifice?

The true person must come from within
We can create the virus to destroy the sin
And people are the creatures of their own vice
But at what cost is the sacrifice?

CEMETERY

I walk along the road of positivity
On a bright clear Summer's day
My heart is full of levity
I have so much I want to say

I light a cigarette, it gives me a warm feeling
My heart is open for all to see
Life's expectations are so appealing
I feel like a brand new me

My heart is quiet, my brain is at peace
My soul now feels no fear
I long for this moment never to cease
I relinquish the clouds of despair

The weather changes, the sun disappears
The warm peaceful feeling is now cold
All the holes have now become squares
And the Gladiator is no longer bold

My heart closes, my cigarette goes out
The expectations become a dark cloud
All positive thoughts are now a doubt
As the Devil corners me with a shroud

The world crumbles beneath my feet
I disappear in a world without sound
My negative thoughts will no longer retreat
From the helplessness from which I'm bound

WISHMASTER

He listens to the sunshine
He walks without a spine
He watches the music
He is indelible, he is intrinsic

He is within, he is without
He hears the silence, he feels the shout
He writes without a pen
He was now, he's now then

He listens to people's pain
He thinks without a brain
He listens to the colours change
He gets close but out of range

He walks on air
He grips hold of despair
He reads without eyes
He reads truth from lies

MIRRORED FLOOR

Walking on a mirrored floor
Reflections of where I've been before
Looking down it seems so wrong
My extended legs no longer strong

Walking on a mirrored floor
Reflections show me a different door
Looking down I see the ceiling
I get a feeling of double dealing

Walking on a mirrored floor
Reflections show me the final score
Looking down I see my immediate past
No tomorrow and a day that doesn't last

SILENT VOICES

Silent voices in the night
Silent whispers in the day
They come to give their fright
They come to block your way

Silent voices in your dreams
Silent whispers in your head
They come with menacing schemes
They come with a feeling of dread

Silent voices in your life
Silent whispers in the air
They come to give you strife
They come to make you swear

Silent voices are the boss
Silent whispers in your bones
They come without any moss
They come like rolling stones

BECAUSE OF LOVE

Because of love
There is no ending
No need to be alone
There is no pretending

Because of love
There is no resistance
No need to surrender
There is no persistence

Because of love
There is no fear
No need for excuses
There is no despair

Because of love
There is no protection
No need for signs
There is no direction

BEHIND CLOSED DOORS

Who knows what lies
Behind the eyes of the despair?
Who can really tell
The hell and the fear
Behind closed doors?

Who knows the emotion
Behind the devotion and cares?
Who can really hide
The pride and the tears
Behind closed doors?

Who knows the deceit
Behind the sweet smelling roses?
Who can really judge
And begrudge the poses
Behind closed doors?

MR KNOW-IT-ALL

How far have you been?
Are you still there?
Have you found the round peg
That fits the square?

When you look in the mirror
Can you see your eyes
Does the reflection you see
Give cause for surprise?

When you walk on people
Are your feet on the ground?
Is your tongue the only weapon
And your voice the only sound?

Do you measure yourself
By all things materialistic?
Are the veins of others
To you unrealistic?

How far can you see
From your narrow-minded space?
When you look in the mirror
Do you change your face?

So where have you been
Through my struggle and strife?
Where have you been
In your supersonic life?

IN A GARDEN

I sat in a garden
And this is what I saw
Nature in its splendour
A life without a flaw

Roses in full bloom
A smile upon their face
Different shades of green
Filling in the space

The sun smiled warmly
Right across the lawn
As the cat rolled over
Just about to yawn

The birds in the sky
Were happy to be free
And the only thing that rained
Was a cloud of tranquillity

I sat in a garden
Me, myself and I
Caught in a magical time warp
Below a placid sky

WITHIN OR WITHOUT

When your wing is broken
And you fall to the floor
When the hounds come hunting
And moan upon your door
Are you within or are you without?

When the penny drops
And the glass shatters behind you
When the hands of time run out
And sympathy becomes untrue
Are you within or are you without?

When you can't hear the thunder
And the lightning blinds your eyes
When helping hands become a hindrance
And smiling faces are just a disguise
Are you within or are you without?

When the sea feels totally calm
And the sand is very wet
When you've got money to spend
And you're still in debt
Are you within or are you without?

When you believe in your fate
And that everything is a test
When you're right up the front
And you feel second best
Are you within or are you without?

HORSEMAN

A man in a cape came to me
His eyes glistening red
He rode on a horse I could not see
And this is what he said
Stand back and have no regret
Be free of emotional debt
Grow old but stay young
Stand and watch and hold your tongue
All you see is but an illusion
Truth lies beyond confusion
Catch the wind and hear the voices
Fate is disguised in many choices
All that glitters is not gold
And a story ends but is not told
You may be ugly, you may be handsome
You may be loved and held for ransom
The clock will tick past many seconds
As countdown comes and time beckons
You may like a poem, you may like a song
Life may be short but eternity is long
Tidal waves will sweep away your mind
And a wandering soul is hard to find
Detach yourself from all the pains
Jump on my horse and grab the reins

SMILE

When nothing goes your way
And unwanted guests just stay
When the machine swallows your money
And the joke on you isn't very funny
Look in the mirror and smile

When all your efforts are in vein
And the feeling in your head is called pain
When words of wisdom become confusion
And the light that shines is just an illusion
Look into your soul and smile

When cupid pulls his bow and flirts
And you are the only one that hurts
When years of patience begins to run out
And you open your mouth but cannot shout
Look into the darkness and smile

When the glass before you needs a refill
And the brain in your head needs another pill
When you feel you owe nobody anything
And it's hard to tell Winter from the Spring
Look within yourself and smile

When you don't know where you're headed
And everything you've believed in is now shredded
When all you feel is only felt by a few
And your reflection is someone you once knew
Look in the direction of a smile

THE RISING SUN

Look up my sleeve
What does it show?
Does what you see
What you know?

The dawn suddenly awakes
With yesterday's mistakes
Still to be solved
The rising sun smiles
But there's so much to be solved

Look up my sleeve
What does it conceal?
Does what you see
What you feel?

God raises the dead
From their sleeping bed
Only to be confused
The rising sun smiles
But someone's not amused

Look up my sleeve
What does it reveal?
Does what you see
What you steal?

Tomorrow becomes today
That once was yesterday
And no one seems to care
The rising sun smiles
But no one seems aware

THANKFUL

When I was young
I spoke with a loose tongue
I walked the path of non-believers
And mixed in the company of deceivers

I entered the world of drink and drugs
I mixed with undesirables and thugs
I walked in darkness even though it was day
I was the main character in every play

When I was young I could shout
And my decisions were made with doubt
I constantly took the train to ecstasy
And the future was just another galaxy

I had to be king of the boys
And the only peace I got was noise
I woke up in the morning and never thought twice
And my fate depended on the roll of the dice

I could make gold out of mud
And the only rush was in my blood
I never stumbled and kept on my feet
And everyone I met, I wanted to meet

Everything I did was just a matter of fact
And every scenario was no fake act
But now I'm thankful for every new day
I'm very thankful for the stay of execution

ROBOTS

We're all prisoners
Held against our will
We're all empty vessels
That never have their fill

We're all shackled
And held in our little cell
We're all kept in the dark
Like water in the well

We're all governed
By politics and religion
We're all part of the system
Democratic but without decision

We're all gagged
And taxed on what we say
We're part of the same dream
Existence is the game we play

We're all robots
With micro-chips in our head
We're all headed in the same direction
Some are living, some are dead

HOTEL

I've walked through the snow
With nowhere to go
And frozen to the bone
I've felt the pain
Of the heavy rain
And the feeling of being alone

I'm checking out
Of this hotel
I've many complaints
But no one to tell

I've reaped what I've sowed
I'd paid what I've owed
And my slate is clean
I've felt the regret
Of being in debt
And the burden of being mean

I'm checking out
Of this hotel
I want some attention
But there is no bell

I've spoken to many ears
I've conquered so many fears
And watched people disappear
I've searched an infinity
For my lost identity
And the reason for being here

I'm checking out
Of this hotel
I have the magic answer
But cannot find the spell

ALIVE

Stillborn by choice
Clinging to my voice
The roads of rock
May have stopped the clock
But I'm happy to be alive

Plans of mice and men
Thoughts of now and then
The sound of rats
May have scurried the cats
But I'm happy to be alive

The missing moon
Appears so soon
The passing of yours
May have left their tears
But I'm happy to be alive

Still silent by choice
Born without a voice
The Gods that dictate
May have been too late
But I'm happy to be alive

ANYONE FOR TENNIS?

Black tennis balls
Bouncing off my head
Like greased lightning
Serving up aces of dread

They come thick and fast
Leaving no space for doubt
I return service with instinct
Even though the balls are out

They sting through the air
As I dig deep into reserve
I move swiftly to the net
And return each menacing serve

Like demons on a mission
They come flying over the net
Blocking out my vision
To take my game and set

Dark clouds simmer above
The Devil's on the loose
I'm fighting back defeat
And now the score is deuce

Drop lobs over the net
Happy to make a catch
I'm stretching myself to the limit
For that game, set and match

DON'T TURN AROUND

Don't turn around
I heard someone say
Because what you know
Will drift slowly away

Don't turn around
If you're caught in a spell
Look for a church
Listen for the bell

Don't turn around
I heard someone shout
Because what you feel
Will always be doubt

Don't turn around
If you're in a dream
Look for an exit
Listen to the scheme

Don't turn around
I heard someone mime
Because what you see
Will be passing time

Don't turn around
If you're feeling afraid
Just look ahead
And follow the parade

IN BETWEEN

When breakfast is over
And all you look forward to is lunch
Is there nothing in between
Not even a hunch?

What becomes of the time unfilled?
What becomes of the milk unspilled?
What becomes of the time in between?
Is it a canvas without a scene?

When the day is over
And all you look forward to is night
Is there nothing in between, not even light?

What becomes of the thoughts in your head?
What becomes of the words not said?
What becomes of the space in between?
Is it a film no one has seen?

CALL FOR PEACE

Put down the gun
Take up the pen
Sit round the table
Shake hand with a friend
Diffuse the bombs
Change violence to words
Let's see hatred end

Put away the masks
Replace them with smiles
Join hands together
Across the miles
Let Ghandi's words
Flow across the table
In tongues of different styles

Spit out hatred swallow the pride
Search the soul
Leave nothing to hide
Make words replace bullets
Let common sense prevail
And let the heart decide

Release the suffering
Whether Arab or Jew
Become a common denominator
Let one and one be two
Remove the dividing boundaries
Make history feel proud
Give mankind its due

BEHIND THE...?

On the dark cold lifeless morning, herds like cattle rolled in on tracks on a one-way ticket, lambs to the slaughter, already drained of life.
Empty eyes denoting empty stomachs never to be filled again.
The final screams in the final solution heralding the end of a miserable existence.
The burning smell of flesh of the old and young is the only cooking that fills the nostrils.
And when the screaming ceased, was it a sign that many had escaped through the chimneys?
The bewildered eyes of the little ones captured forever on film, dressed in stripes, just numbers, tortured for experiments, not knowing what they really were.
What kind of mirrors did their torturers look into?
At liberation many were saved but many minds destroyed forever,
so evil won in the end.
Those with no will left and riddled with disease were the lucky ones who denied and escaped if only the satisfaction of their executioners.
What kind of mind, what kind of conscience makes so many the guardians of hell?
Where do you begin to understand such mentality?
What medication or therapy do you give to the survivors to ease their daily nightmares and documentary that never goes away?
What words or feelings can erase such Post Traumatic Stress?

FOOD AND DRINK FOR THOUGHT

Coriander curries my favour
It heats my blood with flavour
A chicken Jal Freezy
Slips down just as easy
Giving satisfaction to savour

There's nothing like a Darjeeling
That has to be drunk with feeling
And in every plantation
It's the ladies of the nation
That make this drink so appealing

A chicken chow mein or special fried rice
Chicken, pork balls, king prawns and spice
Come with sweet and sour
Is a guarantee it's going to be nice

Whether Christian, Jedi or Jew
Spiritualist, Muslim or Hindu
There's nothing more refine
Than a good quality wine
Or whatever spiritual brew

TOOK A HIKE

Took a hike to the river
To watch the seagulls fly
Took time out to deliver
My ego to the sky

Took a hike to the park
To watch the children play
To listen to the dogs bark
And have nothing to say

Took a hike to the celebration
To watch the joy unfold
Took time out for deliberation
And the feeling of being bold

Took a hike to discover
To watch and to learn
To listen to my sister and brother
Without any bridges to burn

Took a hike to see the fox
To watch something cunning
Took time out of my box
To observe something stunning

Took a hike to the hereafter
To watch my children grow
To listen to their laughter
And regret what I know

ODDS AND FRIENDS

Sober or unsteady
I'm always ready
And willing to be nice
Just a phone call
From a stone wall
Or even a block of ice

You know my number
You know where I live
I ask for nothing
Just willing to give

Low or high
I'm always on stand-by
And always willing to speak
Either a Saturday
Or even a Sunday
Or even during the week

I always make the step
I always have to fall
I always make the journey
I always make the call

Happy or miserable
I'm always visible
And willing to entertain
I'm not that far
By foot or by car
Or even by the train

I don't need your signature
There's no need to pretend
There's no need to be odd
All you have to be is a friend

LIFE AND DEATH

The veil of life and death
It's an invisible veil
And as we pass through it without knowing
Time stands still for a moment
And then begins again
As we become a distant memory
And as one door closes
And another opens
We have to let go
Side by side
We walk life's road
Until we walk alone
We cannot keep what is not ours
And as we disappear down another road
No more judgement
No more hurt
Can ever reach us now

SOMETHING SPIRITUAL

All faiths are of one origin
They're many branches in the same tree
All roads lead to the beginning
Spiritual journeys always come free

Different colours are all but one
There are many clouds that form the rain
All footsteps follow one path
Across a spiritual plain

Different hearts all beat the same
There are many armies with only one goal
All journeys take the same road
A spiritual path through the soul

We are all but one Exodus
There are many waves in the ocean
Whichever direction we decide to go
It's all a spiritual motion

WHY?

Why chase shadows
When there's no one there?
Why feel feelings
Just out of despair?

Why face problems
When they're not yet arrived?
Why feel envy
For those who have survived?

Why chase clouds
If it's bound to rain?
Why feel the fire
If it causes you pain?

Why face the devil
When your time's not yet come?
Why feel anger
Because you're not like some?

Why chase dreams
When there's no guarantees?
Why feel so generous
When there's no one to please?

Why face the future
When you're riddled with guilt?
Why feel like crying
When the milk has spilt?

Why chase rainbows
When there's a total eclipse?
Why feel like kissing
If there aren't any lips?

ARE YOU?

Are you feeling better
Now you're feeling better?
Are you happy
Now you can write a letter?

Are you feeling free
Now you're feeling free?
Are you ecstatic
You can now actually see?

Are you looking ahead
Now you're looking ahead?
Are you relieved
You are no longer dead?

Are you feeling high
Now you're feeling high?
Are you satisfied
You're not passed your sell by?

Words and feelings like traumatised trees
Can scatter everywhere like helpless leaves

WE

We are here
For what you want us to be
You can tie us up or you can set us free
We are here
Forever at your command
You can make us sit or you can make us stand

We are the problems you can solve
We are the options you can choose
We are the questions you can resolve
You alone can change our views

We are here
Centre stage for your pleasure
Our hard work is your total leisure
We are here
Forever in your debt
You can make us feel good or make us regret

We are the signs of your direction
We are the loose ends you join together
We are the outcome of your rejection
You determine if we're now or never

MAN AT THE TOP

Let me help you send the man at the top
If you feel like falling I'll help you to stop
Give me your hand and I'll guide you through
For I am here to help only you
My door is always open for I am the King
Whatever your problem don't hesitate to walk in
Equal opportunities is what I'm about
I am here to listen and disperse your doubt

We carry your interests in our heart
We always have from the very start
There is nothing we cannot do for you
Our interests are all honest and true

Let me help you, said the man in the suit
If you've lost your way I'll find you a route
Give me your trust and I won't lead you astray
For I am the guide to lead your way
My door is always open for we are a team
We share the future of the company dream
Our policy is to replace the old with the new
The caring organisation that cares only for you

We listen to your ideas and we all take note
We're all one family in one big boat
We've crossed many waters and seen many a moon
If I'm not in my office I'll get back to you soon

YOUR HEART

Listen to your heart
It's been with you from the start
Listen to your heroes
They've already been there

Change your world if you must
Your heart is the one to trust
Listen to the voices
They've heard it all before

Listen to your heart
Even if it tears you apart
Listen to your inner voice
It knows who you are

Change your world to suit you
Your heart will always see you through
Listen to your feelings
They have been there before

Listen to your heart
Before its time to depart
Listen to your footsteps
Before you lose your way

HIDING

Hiding in your shell
Can you really tell
If you're in heaven or hell?

Are the demons under your bed
The ones who want you dead?
Are they what you really dread?

Hiding in your hole
Do you hear the bells toll
As the devil takes your soul?

Are your hidden secrets locked away
For away from the light of day
Where your tortured soul will have to pay?

Hiding in your mind
Do you really hope to find
The life you've left behind?

Are people out to mistreat you
To hold you down and beat you
Or do they only want to greet you?

I STUMBLE

Hello my friend
I see you through the mist
As I stumble to the vineyard
Of this mixture I can't resist

The heavy smoke
Blinds me from the view
As I stumble through the words
Spoken by so many to so few

A bag of emotions
Weighs heavy on my shoulder
As I stumble through the files
Desperately looking for my own folder

Look into my eyes
Beyond the glaze of a warm shelter
As I stumble down the hill
Into an oblivious helter-skelter

A token gesture
Slips through me like a dose of salts
As I stumble to regain my dignity
And reflect on society's faults

Hello my friend
I see you through tinted eyes
As I stumble back in time
Looking for a brand new disguise

LIFETIME

I've been on many a long road
I've carried many a heavy load
For a lifetime
I've seen people cry
And watched them die
For a lifetime
I've suffered the envy of people's dreams
I've travelled through swamps and streams
For a lifetime
I've been praised and slated
Made to feel outdated
For a lifetime
I've bridged the gap made by fools
Laid myself bare inside their schools
For a lifetime
I've accepted lies
As part of a disguise
For a lifetime
I've been forced to the edge of no return
Made to leap in order to learn
For a lifetime
I've seen the sun set
On many a regret
For a lifetime
I've followed the light from the eyes of the blind
I've felt many colours inside my mind
For a lifetime
I've been taught to pray
And what not to say
For a lifetime
I've walked the streets of the rich and poor
But it takes a lifetime to find the right door

BEWARE

If you think your troubles
Are all behind you
And the iced cake
Is easy to slice through
If the sun shines each and everyday
Beware of the shadow that leads you astray

If you think bad luck
Is all in your mind
And that your fate
Is so easy to find
If everyone's smile seems true
Beware of the vision that surrounds you

If you think that night
Follows the day
And that happiness
Is but a touch away
If all you see is all you know
Beware of the soul that goes with the flow

DECISIONS

You cherish a thought
You perish a thought
You cast your net
And cast your doubt

Decisions depend
On the throw of the dice
Whether you throw once
Or whether you throw twice

You feel the need
You feel the greed
Slow the mind or let it speed
Stem the flow or let it bleed

Decisions depend
On the state of mind
Whether to move forward
Or whether to stay behind

You change your clothes
You re-arrange your clothes
You set your sails
You set your bails

Decisions rule
In a world of delusion
Whether you vote once
Or twice in confusion

You feel the glow
You feel the know
Slow it down or let it flow
Kill the thought or let it grow

LOVE IS

Love is just a kiss away
Hate is just a miss away
And every losing streak
Drowns the words you want to speak

When your nerves are all broken
And each and every word is a token
The breakdown takes you by surprise
And you become the consolation prize

Love is just a feel away
Hate is just a steal away
And each painful feeling
Is only a wound that is healing

When your feelings are under the thumb
And each and every emotion becomes numb
The silence suddenly becomes loud
And you become a passing cloud

Love is just a stab away
Hate is but a grab away
And every single motion
Is drowned in a stormy ocean

When your blood suddenly turns cold
And your heart no longer feels bold
The question now becomes unsolved
And destiny leaves you unresolved

ROOM FOR THOUGHT

The walls drip with sweat
The mirror cracks with stress
The room closes in like a net
And the ashtrays are a mess

The carpets are like stone
My footsteps seem extra lazy
My blood freezes to the bone
My thoughts are extremely crazy

The curtains draw their own conclusion
The windows have their own pain
Whatever I think, is an illusion
Is this what they call insane?

The clock says time is running out
Each tick explodes in my head
The silence echoes like a shout
The soft sun feels like lead

The pictures on the wall speak
Framed by artists of vision
They are strong where I am weak
Trapped by invisible bars of my prison

Plants stand tall in the room
Anchored firm by their solid roots
Even though they absorb the gloom
They don't wear lead-filled boots

THEY

They sit on the fence
A leg on either side
Hedging their bets
Ready to change direction
Like a leaf in the wind
You will always spot them
Leopards never change
Their words are very convincing
But their windows tell a different story
They're all qualified in maths
But their figures never add up
They wear sheep's clothing
Until you get too close
They always call first
When they toss a coin
They face you with
Sincere words
And leave wounds in your back
They offer you fair play
While holding their cards
Close to their chest
They are full of directions
That lead you back
To the beginning
They comfort your disadvantage
And give you an advantage
Then they create their advantage
From your misadvantage
They crown themselves
Your friend in need
Here today
But gone tomorrow

THE STORM

The emotional tide is turning
The smell of fear is everywhere
The hungry sharks are circling
The clouds have outstaged the sun
The wind is kicking in fury
Waves of despair are rising
The friendly lifebuoy has deserted
The current moves like electricity
A storm is brewing fast
Waves crash through my head
The stinging rain blinds me
Lightning strikes me more than once
Throw me a line
I've got that sinking feeling
It's hard to communicate
When you're drowning
The distress call goes unheard
This is the storm before the calm

STILL I SEARCH

I have travelled many miles
Crossed many barriers
I have seen many sights
And felt much hatred
I have battled with demons
Shook hands with angels
And stumbled many times
I have felt the pain of others
And comforted so many
I have been welcomed by enemies
And isolated by friends
I have been to the edge
And looked down many times
I have shared the lives of many
From one existence to another
I have given myself to others
And asked nothing in return
I have carried many a burden
Up many a rocky road
I have judged so many
And been judged in return
I have gained so much
And lost much, much more
I have travelled through the Twilight Zone
Where mortals have feared to tread
I have followed my gut feelings
And completely lost my way
I've been chased by my shadow
And ended up at the beginning
Still I have to travel
Along many a weary road
Still I search for a vision
To tell me why I search

NO POINT

There's no point putting up signs
If love is blind
There's no point talking
If it falls on deaf ears

We rely on each other so much
A few pleasant words, a tender touch
A gentle smile to flutter the heart
A genuine regret when we depart

There's no point reaching out
If there's no one there
There's no point in running
If there's nowhere to go

We all need a ray of hope
Some comfort to help us cope
A genuine touch from a helping hand
To turn the stone into sand

There's no point seeking
If there's nothing to find
There's no point hoping
If there are no guarantees

WIND OF CHANGE

My worldly possessions have gone up in smoke
Now I know that life is but a joke
It was a hard lesson that had to be learnt
It was a respect that had to be earnt

Now from the ashes I must turn the page
And cool the fires of a burning rage
And from the debris I must reclaim
The scorched letters of my name

The wind has blown my past away
It is scattered around me every day
My hopes, my dreams, my longing desire
Have turned into a raging soul on fire

We think we make the road we walk
The ideas, the feelings, the words we talk
We are the blind, deaf and the crippled of the earth
Lost in space from the time of our birth

How easy the wind of change can turn
Like the life that ends up in an urn

WHAT GROUND ROUND

Arrows of hatred may pierce the heart
From a previous time, just waiting to start
Invisible weights may sit on your shoulder
A debt from youth to someone older
We are but seconds in every minute
And what goes round comes round

It's hard to be judged but easy to judge
It's easy to lose sight and hold on to a grudge
Life is short but we are tall
Stumbling in the dark only to fall
We are but pawns in a game of chess
And what goes round comes round

Words of wisdom are lost in the breeze
We see the leaves but not the trees
We see the ocean but not the fury
When we become the judge and jury
We are but seasons that come and go
And what goes round comes round

The invisible knife stabs far and wide
Leaving a wound that's hard to hide
Words like knives can cut very deep
Like a nightmare that haunts your very sleep
We are but tops spinning for a while
And what goes round comes round

THE LOVE INSIDE

The love inside me
Stands frozen
No amount of heat
Can ever melt it
Frozen in time
For all to see
Forever motionless
In a moving world
The love inside me
Waits patiently
No amount of words
Can ever move it
Forever frozen
In a warm heart
Standing firm
In a restless body
The love inside me
Will never leave
Waiting for the future
To set it free

HISTORY

The world is disintegrating
Splinters of glass scatter far and wide
People are too busy hating
To find true love inside

History repeats itself in the same story
Cities of blood drenched in glory

Pretty flowers no longer grow
Sheets of fire burn flesh and scar
Barren lands will always show
Where man has progressed so far

History is a disease spreading its source
No one can change its moving course

Streets are filled with empty hope
Lost souls overshadowed by fears
No longer will they be able to cope
Dreaming in their sadness and tears

History looks but it cannot see
Blinded by its own intensity

And when the mayhem ceases
And no one can hear a sound
Who will pick up the pieces
And where will peace be found?

History is what we were yesterday
It's what we will be tomorrow,
It's what we are today

BEAST

Frozen in the dark
A shadow with no emotion
An unforgiving presence
That lurks deep in the mind

Creeping in the dark
A motion with no feeling
Empty of all guilt
That makes fate so hungry

Planning in the dark
A soul with no light
A selfish ego at play
That keeps one step ahead

Feeling in the dark
An echo with no voice
An angry kind of bitterness
That makes time stand still

Whispering in the dark
A life with no future
A hunter being hunted
That leaves its footprints behind

Dying in the dark
A beating heart with no pulse
A short circuit in progress
That feeds on the smell of fear

RUN

Run fast, the Devil's on the loose
The slower you get, the tighter the noose
Run fast despite the squeals
Don't look back, there's fire on your heels

Run and don't think back
For you were the joker in the pack
Run from the Prince of darkness and hell
While you still have a story to tell

Run fast the Devil's at your door
He's on the roof, he's under the floor
Run fast despite the screams
Before nightmares take over your dreams

Run and don't even blink
For you are the missing link
Run while you're still earthbound
While your feet are still on the ground

RUNAWAY TRAIN

The rumbling ravenous train
Hurtles relentlessly to let off steam
Crashing crazily along the hard
Hell bent tracks
Terrified, totally out of control
Bounding breathlessly beyond reach
Destined for devastation, electric currents
Burning its brain
Its mad mental wheels now a blinding blur
Screaming silently by, its aching, agonising body
Shakes, rattles and rolls
Bending, burning and blistering into
A nowhere, no-man's land
Menacing miles free of all punishing pain
Pass in the wink of an eye
At this particular point in the
Torment of time, the devil's destination
Is terrifying and totally unknown

CIRCUMSTANCES

Happy feelings all turned sour
One minute seems like an hour
Fruitful times all turned bad
When all the smiles turn sad

The spirit within is totally shredded
While Cupid's arrow remains embedded
True feelings remain deep seated
Burnt out, tired and depleted

When total acceptance becomes isolation
Kind words come as no consolation
When fate slams the door in your face
Plunging you into a world of disgrace

All future plans become rejected
When life becomes the unexpected
Plunged into a dark alien wilderness
Filled with cold stark reality and bitterness

Tears flow like a river deep inside
The drowning sensation becomes hard to hide
Like a bolt of lightning from above
Splitting the seal of true love

Evil raises its head to destroy
The strong foundation built of joy
Snatched from the hand in the blink of an eye
And the only question left is – why?

LIVE AND LEARN

You must have learnt something
In all those years...
Through the despairs, fears and tears
With so many people on your back
And no one giving a little slack

Evil spirits shake the tree
Where we all sit on the brink
We are the branches of humanity
Waiting eventually to sink

You must have seen something
In your eyes...
Through the cries, lies and spies
With so many people under your skin
And all their excuses running thin

Tossing and turning in our dreams
God shows us his mighty fury
We must not forget that our schemes
Will be our judge and jury

SPIRIT

Spirit is spirit
You can't tie it down
It has no smile
It has no frown
It moves like clouds
It rests like the night
It has no roots
It has no sight

Spirit is invisible
It cannot be intimidated
It cannot be captured
It cannot be impersonated
It speaks with no tongue
It has no brain
It feels no remorse
It feels no pain

Spirit is feeling
It lurks inside
It goes when it wants
It comes back like the tide
It's part of a force
It comes from within
It has no soul
It's neither Yang nor Yin

CROSSROADS

Standing at the crossroads
Waiting for a new affliction
The signs that direct you
Lead you to a new crucifixion

The weight of conscience gets heavier
With all the milk you've spilt
Freedom of the soul comes only
With a complete loss of guilt

Love is a colourful world
Suspended in a misty air
It has no solid body
And doesn't even care

The hustling world of make believe
Draws the unchained spirit to play
The world of self-gratification
Leads your soul astray

Happiness comes very cheap
In the daylight toils of sweat
It gives no vision of tomorrow
When today is filled with debt

Standing at the crossroads
Stripped bare and revealed
The signs that once led you
Is a life now signed and sealed

REFLECTION

I pass you on the street
And look into your eyes
And the person I meet
Is me in disguise

A corridor of ideas
From which to chase
The dark side of tears
That has no bruise

I see a picture of me
Reflected through you
I don't like what I see
But I can't hide what's true

A world of envy and scorn
From which beauty reigns
A twin image born
From joy and pains

I am the person within you
No matter what your culture
Whether old or new
We are the perfect sculpture

A world stronger than fiction
Mirrors through your smile
An existence without restriction
An inverted kind of style

Are you seeing me
As I see your reflection?
Is your soul as free
As our mutual reflection?

MY CLOUD

What is pleasure
But a blink in space?
What is leisure
But a time and place?

Don't sit on my cloud
It is reserved for me
When I'm covered in a shroud
Then the cloud will be free

What is might
But a negative view?
What is light
But a day that's new?

Don't give me excuses
For your own guilt
My soul refuses
What yours has spilt

What is life
But a burden on the shoulder?
What is strife
But wisdom that is older?

Don't cover my eyes
With painted overviews
When beneath the surface lies
Headlines of yesterday's news

What is philosophy
But wolves disguised as sheep?
What is atrocity
But you pretending to be asleep?

A PART OF ME

I class myself as advantaged
Reaching the souls of people
I'm the soft centre
Who's really hard
My vision is beyond any steeple

I am he who can perceive
Everything written in my blood
I can lose and never retrieve
Like a city washed by flood

I can tear my soul to pieces
Within the confines of normality
I am my saviour who never ceases
To break the etiquette of formality

I class myself as a non-entity
Who feeds on other people's bluff
I am the hardcore of society's pity
Whose ego never gives enough

I'm the bitter pill of redemption
Who people find hard to swallow
I cannot give society perfection
When my soul is left fallow

SOMEDAY

Someday will come, I said
Someday was inside my head
Not a lot going, not a lot to say
When it's time to go, you cannot stay

Someday was deep inside
Someday that could not hide
Still I wandered, still I prayed
Feeling very brave but very afraid

Someday the voice will reach me
Someday my eyes will see
Speaking becomes so complex
A movement without a reflex

Someday will leave its mark
Someday will leave a spark
The circle now becomes a square
And there's no escape anywhere

Someday will come to an end
Someday will be my friend
Not a lot of love, not much serenity
Now the jury's out, will there by any dignity?

FIRE

I feel like a horse
In a burning stable
My vision s very poor
But my feelings are able

The flames lick me
Taunt me and burn me
My high expectations
Turn away and spurn me

My eyes can only see
What is blinded by smoke
My fight syndrome has eluded
And my words make me choke

I feel I'm in hell
No longer in command
I've nowhere to run
I'm unable to stand

The flames suck me
Drain me and derange me
My once clear vision
Changes and re-arranges me

My soul is burning
As my body starts to stumble
My fight syndrome melts
As I start to crumble

THE FORCES

This tidal wave
This dark cloud
Why do they come to my door?
Why does it wash away
All that's done?
Why does it black out
The rising sun?

The spiritual lows dictate
People are the creations of their fate
What you see, is not really true
And to get over you have to go through

This earthquake
This hurricane
Why do they come to my door?
Why does it disrupt
The even ground?
Why does it blow away
The peaceful sound?

The spiritual laws decree
People create their own destiny
You cannot swim without getting wet
There is no margin for regret

FOR ONCE

Let me do my own thing
Let me hear my heart sing
For once
Let me fight my revolution
Let me find my evolution
For once

Change can be strange
When it's cold
History is a lesson
Only for the bold

Let me do my own schooling
Let me do my own fooling
For once
Let me go where no one has gone
Let me sing my own song
For once

Fate is a weight
Carried by few
Tomorrow is a hope
That might come true

Let me reach my own end
Let me find my own friend
For once
Let me reach my own course
Let me feel my own force
For once

Believing is deceiving
Wherever you are
Existence is near
No matter how far

GOOD MORNING

The outside world hurts
Like the simple choice
Of choosing shirts

The inside walls crack
Like the sudden jolt
Of a wake up smack

The outside world blinds
Like the losing grip
Of insane minds

The inside darkness rages
Like the sudden birth
Of many ages

The outside world wakes
Like the deceptive tongues
Of venomous snakes

FAMILY

My dad said no
My mum said yes
My sister was silent
And I had to guess

My dad was the pen
My mum was the page
My sister and I
Were the words of rage

My dad was strict
My mum was kind
My sister followed
And I was blind

My dad was strong
My mum was weak
My sister and I
Were the losing streak

My dad said stop
My mum said go
My sister was bewildered
And I didn't know

My dad was right
My mum refrained
My sister and I
Were completely drained

My dad was weak
My mum was bold
My sister was young
And I was old

IF ONLY

If only peace could reign
And I could feel the end
If only I had
One true friend

If only I could see
Where I go wrong
If only my words
Could be a song

If only I could hold on
And not lose grip
If only I could die
And enjoy the trip

If only shadows could speak
And cast their hidden face
If only I could
Vanish without a trace

If only I could see
Beyond the smoke
If only I could speak
And not have to choke

If only I could reclaim
What is mine
If only I had
A solid spine

I AM ME

I've been shakened, awakened
And taken
I've been clipped, stripped
And whipped

I've been bound, clowned
And drowned
I've been loved and I've been hated
I've been praised and I've been slated

I've been rejected, dejected
And suspected
I've been hated, underrated
And deflated

I've been led, bled
And left for dead
I am a product, I am a community
I exist, I am me

LOST

Don't follow me
Or you'll be lost
It's a chilly wind
That brings the frost

The night brings darkness
As do my eyes
The fright makes heroes
From every disguise

Don't ask me the way
Or you'll be lost
It's a hard life
That shows its cost

The day brings light
As do my feelings
The way ahead is full
Of double dealings

Don't ask me for strength
Or you'll be weak
It's an ill wind
That makes a freak

The morning brings glory
As do my fears
The dawning of age
Is full of tears

ODE TO WINE

Let tomorrow take care of itself
Let the wine fill
Your belly with rage

Let the sorrow seep through the walls
Let the wine fill
Your body with age

Let today take care of itself
Let the wine spill
And stain your ego

Let the way take care of itself
Let the wine warm
Where no one dares go

Let the night take care of itself
Let the wine drown
The spaces in your head

Let the fright take care of itself
Let the wine raise
The sleeping dead

STARS

Look at the stars
And feel the urge
Feel the motivation
Feel the surge

Sparkling eyes
Speaking volumes
Lighting the way
For witches on brooms

Glitter in space
Against a dark ceiling
Shooting down
A warm feeling

Scattered diamonds
Light up the rockets
Peering through the dark
From empty sockets

PRISONER

Prisoner in a web
Waiting for the tide to ebb
Trapped by a love inside
Washed up by the evening tide

Prisoner of many emotions
Spread across many oceans
A love boat filled to the brim
Overloaded, unable to swim

Prisoner on the edge
Trapped inside a pledge
All washed up and feeling sore
Like the fossils along the shore

Prisoner inside your head
Like rocks on the sea bed
Emotional winds blind the sight
Like passing prisoners in the night

THE WELL

The well of mystery
Overflows each day
Each part of history
Has so much to say

Deep down inside
Where spirits hide
Deep down within
Far away from sin

The well of life
Spills its load
Each and every strife
Becomes a road

Deep down inside
Is the genocide
Deep down within
Is where we begin

The well of existence
Overflows each day
Each part of resistance
Is the game we play

WATCH NOW

Watch now carefully
Let it be
Let go of the rope
That chokes the hope
Of sincerity

Watch now peacefully
Let it grow
Let go of the hate
That grips your fate
And stems the flow

Watch now hopefully
Let it speak
Let go of the chain
That keeps your brain
Constantly weak

Watch now, listen to me
Cast no doubt
Let go of the blunder
That makes you wonder
What it's about

VIEWMASTER

Urban foxes
Letter boxes
Words with nothing to say
Casting nets
Low flying jets
The one that got away
Holiday snaps
Baseball caps
Stuck on away-day trains
Prison cells
Ringing bells
Kids with junky brains
Hypnotherapy
Psychotherapy
A city of all night raves
Blushing brides
Rushing tides
Young and middle-age slaves
Sleeping nations
Preoccupations
Words already omitted
Time and motion
Suntan lotion
Only a few permitted
Car chases
Rat races
Tied up in loose ends
False friends
Suppression
Depression
The customary false friends
Smoking dope,
Kaleidoscope
A mind of ageing bones
Fruity wines,
Neon signs

A host of ancient stones
Rejection,
Dejection
The race of ticking clocks
Daily papers,
Drunken capers
The sound of changing locks
News reviews, Arab and Jew
Everything moving faster
Madness, sadness
It's all in my Viewmaster.

TIME

Thank you for the time
Spent in pleasant company
Thank you for the time
Watching my children grow

All that you see
All that you know
All that is free
Will eventually go

Thank you for the time
Spent in the warmth of the sun
Thank you for the time
When my heart surged with love

All that is grown
All that you cherish
All that is known
Will eventually perish

Thank you for the time
Spent looking at the moon
Thank you for the time
Watching the river flow

All that is earnt
All that is made
All that is learnt
Will eventually fade

Thank you for the time
Spent looking at the flowers
Thank you for the time
Watching the trees grow

All that is desired
All that is a mystery
All that is acquired
Will eventually be history

PERFECT

Such a perfect scene
Ripples in the stream
Peace in its motion
Echoing in the woods

Such a perfect sky
Splashed in paint
Perfection in colour
By an invisible artist

Such a perfect garden
With scents that ease
Welcoming butterflies
Gathering around

Such a perfect night
The moon and stars reign
Trees remain silent
The air is asleep

Such a perfect day
Sunshine warms the soul
Seeping into the bones
Taking away the pain

Such a perfect wine
Slipping down with ease
Opening up visions
That flow through the veins

Such perfect music
Drowns the soul
Suddenly what you feel
Is who you are

Such a perfect end
Problems are dissolving
Feeling like someone else
Is such a boost

AFTER THE EVENT

Look over your shoulder
Are you younger or a little older
After the event?

Are you a spendthrift or a miser?
Are you older or wiser
After the event?

Are your footsteps slow or fast?
Can your spirit really last
After the event?

Does your soul feel pride
When you really have to hide
After the event?

Are your feelings dog tired
When your soul has retired
After the event?

Do you feel slightly worried
When your decisions are hurried
After the event?

NO NEED

No need to fight
No need to prove wrong from right
No need to split hairs
No need to change oblongs to squares

Change is as good as a rest
Is what they say
But the well of inspiration
Has its off day

No need to be bolder
No need to look over your shoulder
No need to be ahead
No need to be a long time dead

Let sleeping dogs lie
Is what they say
But a conscience without resolution
Is one more wasted day

No need to take stock
No need to keep an eye on the clock
No need to wonder why
No need to watch time fly

You reap what you sew
Is what they say
But a land of desolation
Becomes another day

THE CHIEF

Let the chief think
In a brief blink
Of obscurity

Let the motion slow
And the ocean flow
Through eternity

Let him feel the thunder
That comes with blunder
Of insecurity

Let it be what it must
And let him see the thrust
Of reality

Let tomorrow frown
And sorrow drown
Each diversity

Let all who must
Fail to trust
The divinity

Let him feel annoyed
And steal the void
Of insanity

Let the chief reign
On the brief pain
Of his vanity

ADVICE

Listen to advice
And treat it with care
Show me every vice
And I've been there

Keep all your constitutions
Your revolutions
And institutions

Keep you dimensions
Your redemptions
And superstitions

Listen to the expressions
And feel the link
Show the concessions
That make you think

Keep your simplicity
Your complacency
And diversity

Keep what you hear
What you fear
And what you dare

Listen to advice
And treat it with care
Ignore the spice
Of poison and despair

SEARCHING

The loner in his room
Spends his life in the water
Surrounded by fins
And like the prophet of doom
The drunk spends his life
Surrounded by ruins

Everybody's searching for something
Always looking for a direction
Everyone's reaching for something
Always looking for a connection

The child in the class
Spends its life in detention
Listening to voices,
And like the shattered glass
That stands behind you
There are no choices

Everyone' searching for a leader
Always looking for a teacher
Everyone's searching for a wizard
But no one wants a preacher

The model in her pose
Spends her life in focus
Listening to flattery,
And like a river that's froze
The choices become blinkered
And flat as a battery

Everyone's looking for somebody
Always searching in the dark
Everyone's feeling for somebody
Always looking for a spark

SPIRITUAL LAWS

The barking dog that raises the dead
The constant chatter in your head
The alarm bell you always dread
Everything is as it should be

The spiritual laws dictate
You must love everything you hate
What must be must be
Time and tide has to be free

The trapdoor that falls from under you
The guilt that eats you through and through
The luck that's shared with only a few
Everything is as it should be

The spiritual law will reign
You must seek it even in vain
What you lose is not really yours
A long winding road has many doors

THE TRAIN

Pack your bags
And don't be late
Put on your glad rags
The train won't wait

When the train pulls into the station
Make sure you're ready to go
There'll be no time for contemplation
There's so much you need to know

Pack your spares
And put your troubles away
Leave all your cares
The train won't stay

Make sure you're not left behind
When the train gathers speed
There's so much you'll need to find
And nothing you'll ever need

Pack your lunch
And don't be slow
Follow your hunch
Or the train will go

Make sure you go with the flow
When the train pulls away
There's nothing you need to show
And nothing you need to say

HOLOCAUST

Instantaneous karma
Like hot coals
Burns my feet
The neon signs
All say CLOSED
On every street

Instantaneous holocaust
Like resuscitation
Brings me alive
To face the fact
I'm the only one
Left to survive

Instantaneous serum
Like an injection
Fills my blood
The empty streets
Reverberate aloud
With a rushing flood

Instantaneous people
Vanish in a blink
Manic tendencies
Become the soldiers
Trained to make you think
Of invading enemies

Instantaneous armies
Mercilessly taunt you
To stand or fight
The moral issue
Is your only weapon
Wrong or right

Instantaneous death
Opens up the door
To a taunting voice
The only real option
Does God exist
To give you the choice?

BLUEPRINT

The blueprint of our lives only scan the system we can see. Like the iceberg no one tells us there is more underneath.
And those who blindly follow the herd, become the clowns on a tightrope with no safety net.
When the placenta is replaced by cotton wool, future surroundings become a padded cell.
The sounds of time seep through the eye of a needle when you run before you crawl.
And those with glass heads who carry excess baggage of egos are the first to choke on humble pie.
Today's a gamble, tomorrow's a risk and if the dice aren't loaded, the gun most certainly will be. And like the air that's all about, whatever's within will become without.
The laws of nature legislate to cut your cloth to fit the pennies in your pocket.
So let it be written, so let it be done.
And when the signs that say STOP make you feel dyslexic, when the party balloons all burst, it's a sure sign the party's over.
As the world stops on its axis, it's real love that will keep it spinning.

SOME KIND

When your ego is thoroughly broken
And the alarm bells say you are woken
Is this some kind of a token?

When you feel like a contribution
And life becomes an institution
Is this some kind of retribution?

When you feel totally under
And your head is full of thunder
Is this some kind of blunder?

When nobody rings on the phone
And voices change their tone
Is this some kind of comfort zone?

When everything has its own place
And solitude fills as your space
Is this some kind of disgrace?

THERAPY

I'm waiting to see you
As you wait to see me
I'm waiting for you to see
What you can see in me
Tell me what you see
Can you see I'm older?
Do you think I'm bolder?
Do you see the weight on my shoulder?
Are my streets really paved?
Can my soul really be saved?
Are my scenes waiting to be played?
Should I cross myself?
Do I have to boss myself
Or have I lost myself?
Will you put things in my head
To make me feel what I dread
That I'm alive even though I'm dead?
If you look into my window
Will you see sunshine or falling snow?
Does the sign say stop or go?
Does creativity come with a drink?
Is that what you really think
Or am I ahead of you in the eye of a blink?
Is there nothing left but retribution?
Should I be in an institution
Or am I part of an ageing revolution?

WILL YOU?

There will come a time
When nothing matters
As the wind blows
And each leaf scatters.

Will you be there to listen
When I have to plead?
Will you be there to hold my hand
In my time of need?

As time drifts
Like snow on the ground
There will come a time
When there is no sound.

Will you lie beside me
When I need a friend?
Will you cuddle me
Until the end?

There'll be many an image
When I have gone
There'll be many words
And many a song.

Will you move on
And set yourself free?
Will you forget
What used to be?

Of All

The grains of sand
Slip through the hand
And the many visions
Of all those prisons
Become hard to understand

The passing of time
Measures like crime
And each and every word
Of all the stories unheard
Become hard to rhyme

The ageing old bones
Click together like stones
And the measured out miles
Of all those smiles
Become the dulcet tones

The many and the few
Are the old and the new
And those split-second mistakes
Of all realistic fakes
Become part of you

FORGIVENESS

I have many complaints
That would strip the saints
Of their immortality

My feelings vibrate
Everything I hate
In a desolate world

Guilt is the boss
That puts you on the cross
To suffer in silence

What does it take
To be forgiven a mistake
And ask for forgiveness?

VISION

Surrender your soul from the substance within
Destroy the destruction that comes with sin
No need to fear the fear that haunts you
Never deny the love that denies the few

As God is my witness the jury is always out
The sin of all sins casts shadow of doubt
This wonderful world that so many elude
Can only be seen through the blindness of the shrewd

MORTALS

I have reached
Where most mortals fear to tread
I have seen
What most mortals always dread

I have swallowed
What most mortals fear to touch
I have been
What most mortals fear as much

I have loved
When most mortals have been asleep
I have lost
What mortals long to keep

I have preached
What most mortals fear to hear
I have faced
What mortals call despair

BEWARE

Beware of the charlatans
Who take your power
There is more to worry about
Than the midnight hour

Beware of the devils
Who infiltrate your head
There is no emotional substance
To the lies you are fed

Beware of the villains
Who suck you dry
There is more to sweet talk
Than a glint in the eye

Beware of the treadmill
That leads to nowhere
There are only expectations
That fuel your fear

Beware of the sentence
Formed by perfect words
There…

(unfinished)

TOTALLY

Totally detached
Drifting in space
There is no sound
No human race

Totally separated
From family and friends
Sifting through eternity
Looking for an end

Totally segregated
In a box marked fragile
Every single inch
Is equal to a mile

Totally scattered
Files on the floor
There is no sequence
In the system anymore

Totally unearthed
Exposed at last
A castle on the hill
A relic of the past

WEEKEND

Another weekend alone
Memories flood back from the past
A cold chill fills my every bone
Where is the world I thought would last?

Has it crumbled before my feet
Beneath the footsteps of every street?
Where is the vision I thought would never end?
Is it now an illusion I thought was my friend?

Another weekend towers
Suddenly seconds become hours
Truth is now stronger than fiction
As Dutch courage becomes an addiction

Must I choke on swallowing pride
From all the feelings I've been denied?
Not being able to turn back the lock
Presents the soul its inevitable shock

Another weekend crashes
As I pick myself up from the ashes
Burnt out pride becomes a drill
When you have to swallow that bitter pill

And if I should die before I wake
Let's put it down to an inevitable mistake
Drowning in wine and a smoker's cough
Trapped on a merry-go-round and can't get off

WHAT IS THIS?

What tidal wave is this
That takes me under
While my back is turned
Like another page in my life?

What freak wave is this?
What makes me blunder
Each time I face the future
Like a statue pointing out to sea?

What undercurrent is this
That sounds like thunder
Sucking the life force from me
Like a sinking ship in a storm?

What drowning feeling is this
That makes me wonder
Why the tide has turned against me
Like a dysfunctional entity in distress?

LISTEN

Listen to your heart
Love has a whispering voice
Don't let the Devil
Give you a choice

Listen to the signs
It is the way of the force
Don't let the wolf
Change your course

Listen to your feelings
It is the inner you
Don't let the public
Tell you what's true

Listen to the honest
They have no disguise
Don't let jealousy
Cloud your eyes

Listen to the dumb
They have so much to say
Don't let unforgiveness
Block your way

Listen to your freedom
It's the only chance you'll get
Don't let safety
Be your saving net

Listen to yourself
Follow your mind
Don't let the Devil
Make you look behind

CRUCIFIXION

Open the shell
And let the demons out
There can be no illusion
Or confusion
Or room for doubt

Watch the signs as they change direction
Avoid the arrows that bring rejection
Follow the drummer if the beat sounds right
Like the sun that casts a shadow into the night

Open the book
And let everyone read
Let the story unfold
And be told
To the very last deed

Look for blue sky and golden fields
Avoid the swords and blinding shields
Follow your heart to the bitter end
Let the negative feelings become your friend

Open your eyes
And let others see
Let the vision spread
And raise the dead
To set the soul free

Let your soul be the sound people hear
Make your love be the voice people fear
Walking alone is painful, bloody friend
But the pain you shed, will be worth it in the end

ILLUSION

I may look clean
But my soul is black
And all I possess
Will fill only a sack

I may seem sound
But my ego is fragile
I may give an inch
But it measures a mile

I may give you a smile
But inside I'm crying
And the sound you hear
Will only be lying

I may seem happy
But it's what you expect
I maybe a product
But I'm only a reject

I may give you hope
But inside I'm lost
And the vision you see
Comes at a cost

I may be a reflection
But I'm only what's true
I may be flesh and blood
But I'm only you

THEY

They tell you not to criticise
The old and the wise
And to subtract illusion
From total confusion

They tell you not to criticise
The gift of second prize
And that all that's lost
Was worth the cost

They tell you not to criticise
The art of surprise
And what crawls under the skin
Is only the will to begin

They tell you not to criticise
Those who tell you lies
And that all you can reclaim
Is the ashes of your name

They tell you not to criticise
The infiltrating spies
And to be ever so humble
Even though your mind will crumble

They tell you not to criticise
The tormented cries
And that tangled emotions
Become only strangled motions

TWO PEOPLE

I feel like two different people
A church with and without a steeple
I'm on the outside looking in
I'm standing still but I'm in a spin

When it's dark I wish it was light
When it's the day I wish it was the night
I'm two personalities with one ego
The other one I don't really know

I'm one journey on two different roads
I carry one case with two different loads
When I'm high I'm under stress
Who am I is anybody's guess

I feel like two peas in the same pod
Feeling secure but also very odd
One minute I'm slow, then fast as a hare
I seem to be in one place yet everywhere

I want to see but I'm afraid to look
Two stuck pages in the same book
I'm an entity with many forces
One main meal with many courses

ADDICTED

I've been addicted
And lost my mind
I've been restricted
And left for blind

I've seen faces and places
Been misplaced and disgraced
I've met the rich, I've met the poor
Life's a bitch, life's a whore

I've been invited
To come and play
I've been incited
And led astray

I've seen disguises and surprises
Seen the tough and the rough
I've seen the sorrow, I've seen the lies
Life's on borrow, life is wise

I've been addicted
And lost my way
I've been afflicted
And made to pay

DON'T BE SHY

Don't be shy
Don't feel blamed
If there's a tear in your eye
Don't feel ashamed

It's because we care
We carry the weight
Life is not fair
But don't feel hate

Don't be shy
Don't feel small
If you drop from a high
Take the fall

It's because we care
We carry the load
Feel the fear
And walk the road

Don't feel shy
Don't feel blue
Wipe the tear from your eye
Peace is within you

SUMMER

The rising heat
Beneath the feet
Swelters from above
The happy sun
Is having fun
Bathing us with love

Happy smiles
Stretch for miles
And mercury rises
As winter fades
The buckets and spades
Come in many sizes

All around
There's music and sound
And barbeques
Engines belt
And tarmacs melt
Like the winter blues

Sunshine leaches
And sardine beaches
Roads choc-a-bloc
Bodies roast
Making the most
Of the ticking clock

WHAT IS LOVE?

Love is devotion
It's plain to see
A heartfelt plea
A revolution

A simple drop of rain
To ease the pain
The words of a song
To make you feel strong

Love is true
A hate-free zone
When you're alone
And wish to be two

A motion in time
Two words that rhyme
Two beats of a heart
Whether near or apart

Love is strong
It's a way to feel
A spirit of steel
When nights are long

A power within
Born without sin
A simple friend
A life without end

SLUM

No sun shines
In the blighted slums
Only darkness prevails
Until judgement day comes

A pile of bricks
Soaked deep in damp
Keeps people in common
Like a reservation camp

Born into poverty
The last in the link
No rags to riches story
To take them from the brink

Cold empty hearts
Surrender from birth
Empty sockets sink
Deep within the earth

One step forward
And two steps back
The road to envy
Is a familiar track

CONSCIENCE

If six comes before seven
And hell comes before heaven
Then let me out into the city
Where I can feel hate and pity

If cold comes before heat
And bitter comes before sweet
Then let me take all the flack
And the twisted knives in my back

If God is a devil and life's a bitch
If a needle comes before a stitch
Then let the hand of mistrust
Rub my face into the dust

If happiness comes before fright
And day comes before night
Then let me be caught in the snare
Where I can feel my own despair

If a smile comes before a kiss
And torture comes before bliss
Can your feelings be ever true
If you conscience bothers you?

AN EYE

I have an eye
For something that isn't there
If you say it's round
I'll see it square

I have an ear
For a sound that isn't right
If you say it's day
I'll hear the night

I have a notion
For something without feeling
If you find it boring
I'll find it appealing

I have the answer
For what people often fear
If you cannot speak
I'll know what you hear

I have an eye
For something unexpected
If you say it's whole
I'll see it dissected

BEHIND YOU

Why did you have to go
And leave the door wide open?
You could have closed it
Behind you

So many questions
Waiting for a reply
With each passing day
The question is still why?

Why did you have to go
And leave my heart open wide
As you left your shadow
Behind you?
Each day is older
But nothing really new
Locked in a prison
Still waiting for a clue

Why did you have to go
And leave me in such a void
As you left the past
Behind you?

BODYGUARD

I wish I had a bodyguard
Someone to stand by my side
Someone who believes in my ideals
And not take me for a ride

I wish I had a bodyguard
Someone sincere but not smug
Someone who really understands me
And not make me feel like a mug

I wish I had a bodyguard
Someone to clear away the smoke
Someone who believes in just me
And not take me for a joke

I wish I had a bodyguard
Someone different from the rest
Someone who is really genuine
And not make me feel second best

I wish I had a bodyguard
Someone invisible but there
Someone who sees me as round
And not take me for a square

BUTTERFLY

Butterfly
Not a whisper
Not a cry
A pleasing sight
Against the sky
No noisy engine
Needed to fly
No reason
To have to lie
Free to roam
Without a tie
No frustrations
No heavy sigh
Totally calm
No need to try
Quickly flitting
Past the eye
No long life
Soon to die
But happiness lives
In the Butterfly

CARRY ON SOLDIER

He wants to block out his life
Now crippled and short fused
It's all a senseless journey
Totally misleading and confused

He wants to block out his life
The anger that is rising
It's all a pointless cause
Where nothing is really surprising

He wants to block out his life
To stop the constant weeping
It's all just wasted words
Lost in the turmoil of sleeping

He wants to block out his life
The disguised mental rape
It's all a senseless exercise
A freedom with no escape

CLOSE TO ME

There are some things
That are closer to me than others
Despite the passing of time
They remain close to me

The fondness of those memories
Always remain very close
Despite trials and tribulations
They are closer than most

Sometimes I'm very far away
Sometimes I'm nowhere at all
But those special times
Are still very close to me

I drift from day to day
Always in a different world
But those very special moments
Are closer than most

DARK FORCE

Go away dark force
I know you listen
My weakness is strong
And my dullness will glisten

Stay away dark force
I know you hide
My love is strong
And my future is pride

Move away dark force
I know you stalk
My words are strong
And my mind will talk

Walk away dark force
I know you lie
My bond is strong
And my spirit is high

Turn away dark force
I know you hate
My will is concrete
And my concrete is fate

DEEP WITHIN

Jealous eyes
Can make you shout
Painted lies
Can leave a doubt
Deep within your soul

Heartaches you will remember
And all the many kisses
From January to December
Captured in reminiscences
Deep within your mind

All the love you gave
Will become yesterday
No matter how you behave
Nothing will change the day
Deep within your memories

Jealous lies
Will make you weep
Sorrowful eyes
Will leave you deep
Deep within your ego

DON'T CUT THE CAKE

Breaking up is like cutting through that beautiful iced cake
That took so much loving care to make
The love, care and preparation
Now becomes total separation
A gentle thrust from a sharp knife
That cuts deep into your life
If only the cake could stay in its glory
The outcome would be a different story
But it seems that circumstances must prevail
For those whose life has a different tale
Each of us has to do their duty
Even if it means destroying the beauty
Maybe if we could throw away the crutch
Then maybe we could view instead of touch
So look deep into my eyes
And only then will you realise
The passion that's at stake
So please don't cut the cake

EMPTY PEOPLE

Empty voices
With no vision
Empty rooms
In a prison

People dressed
But completely bare
People blind
Forced to stare

Empty people
In a park
Empty memories
In the dark

People dread
But made to talk
People paralysed
Forced to walk

Empty speeches
With no tongue
Empty love
Left unsung

People happy
But full of tears
People will be the same
In a hundred years

FAITH

On one side of the coin
Is Faith
On the other side of the coin
Is doubt
It's not what's outside
Looking in
It's what's inside
Looking out

There's no such thing
As bad weather
Only bad clothing
There's no such person
As the Devil
Only self-loathing

I am now a soldier
I've got myself a gun
I've learnt how to crawl
I've learnt how to run

I know how to hide
I know how to seek
I know how to walk
I know how to speak
I've learnt the art of teamwork
To hold the flag up high
The only thing I have not learnt
Is the proper way to die

FEAR

Fear rising from the stomach, heart, deep inside the mind
Fear from the past, the future and the present
All collectively combined

It's the invisible host of child, man and womanhood
It's the ghosts conveyed by other people
It's psychoanalysed and misunderstood

Cheated by many fathers and many mothers
By brainwashers, leaches and man-made myths
And passed onto sisters and brothers

Like a rabbit caught in the headlights
It's an invisible veil that becomes
A case of what ifs and what mights

MORTALS

I have reached
Where mortals fear to tread
I have seen
What most mortals always dread
I have swallowed
What most mortals fear to touch
I have been
What most mortals fear so much
I have loved
When most mortals have been asleep
I have lost
What mortals long to keep
I have preached
What most mortals fear to hear
I have faced
What mortals call despair

FEEL FREE

You can call me a brass pole
Please feel free
You can call me a grass hole
Please open up to honesty

If you think I care
What you really think
Then your despair
Must be on the brink

You can call me blunt
Please feel free
You can call me a stunt
Please open up sincerity

If you think my sleep
Is disturbed by your fears
Then watch me weep
With crocodile tears

You can call me a brick
Please feel free
You can call me a prize trick
Please open up to complacency

I CAN SHOW YOU

If I could show you
The inside of the minds
Of the people I have known
Then I could show
The insane overload
Of every fuse I have blown

If I could show you
The people I have met
On every conceivable plane
Then I could show you
The inside looking out
That's made society insane

If I could show you
The people I have trusted
At the end of every rainbow
Then I could show
The so-called friends
Who you think you really know

If I could show you
The begging souls
And all I have had to borrow
Then I could show you
The very true meaning
Of people's invented sorrow

If I could show
All those people
I have underestimated
Then I could show you
All the basic follies
That make us all underrated

I CAN'T SAY

I can't say I did
I can't say I didn't
I can't say who is to blame
Maybe I did
Maybe I didn't
Is it worth the humility and shame

Six of one
Half a dozen of the other
It could have been my Father
It could have been my Mother

I can't say I was
I can't say I wasn't
I can't say if I was there
Maybe I was
Maybe I wasn't
Is it really worth a care?

Fifty-fifty
I'm not really sure
Who gives a toss
Whether it's less or more?
I can't say I am
I can't say I am not
I can't say I'll never know
Maybe I am
Maybe I am not
Maybe I'm a solo show

Was I a son
Or was I a daughter
Was I a circle
Or just a quarter?

I PAINT

I paint in words
Like the sound of birds
And the wind in the tress
I paint from the mind
Whatever I can find
Like a passing breeze

The sound of thunder
Is not a blunder
Or part of an entity
I paint the sound
That can only be found
In a person's own destiny

I paint the desire
Of a passionate fire
That burns from the page
I paint with feeling
All that's appealing
And even the rage

How do the birds survive
The chronic winters
And blistering summers?
They cannot strip off
Or even wrap up
In woolly jumpers.

How do the birds survive
When they are hungry
And cannot find food?
Do they give up
Become withdrawn
And go into a mood?

ISOLATION

Isolation is a disease
That spreads like the plague
It produces many changes
Like positive to vague

Isolation is a nightmare
Its control is indiscreet
Its not only indoors
But on every street

Isolation is a stranger
Taking over like day from night
It infiltrates without warning
It changes fight to flight

Isolation is a photograph
A negative of space
A snapshot of a void
That should be a face

Isolation is a penance
Waiting for the tide to turn
I think it's part of Karma
Something we have to learn

I'VE BECOME

I've moved
From one side of the room
To the other
I've become
Some peculiar kind of
Other brother

I've always
Been part of a two
And so confusing
I've become
A different two and
Very amusing

I've moved
From one kind of society
To the other
I've become
Some peculiar kind of
Rejected lover

I've always
Been part of a road
That led to nowhere
I've become
A different dimension
And very aware

MECCA THE BINGO HALL

What are you? said the Priest
I am Satan, said the Beast
Then let me take you by the hand
And place your feet in the Holy Land

I can show you the truth
From your misspent youth
I can change the bad into good
From your misguided parenthood

Whatever you eat, said the Priest
I can turn that into a feast
If you don't know what is false or true
Then I have been chosen to guide you

I can give you absolution
From your years of desolation
I can show you the light and the way
From the path you were forced to stray

Thank you very much but I think I'll pass
I'm far too old to be part of this class
I respect your beliefs as your very own
But I would appreciate it if you left me alone

NO BATTERIES REQUIRED

When your feet come off the accelerator
And you no longer feel tired
It's only then you've passed the test
And there's no batteries required

When your brain switches completely off
And you no longer feel inspired
It's only then you've reached perfection
And there's no batteries required

When all is said and all is done
And you no longer feel wired
It's only then you'll become defused
And there's no batteries required

When your anger becomes quenched
And you no longer feel so tired
It's only then you've reached out
And there's no batteries required

NUCLEAR WASTE

Like Nuclear Waste charred in my head
The taste of my dreams still lingers
A sky of clouds filled with lead
A hand without any fingers

A drought in my brain
Leaves me totally numb
The self-imposed hangover pain
Is all it takes to make me dumb

I was what you are now
Lost in a field of no emotion
When nothing was when or even how
And feeling was without devotion

I was the shadow who was cast
The stranger nobody knew
I was the theory that could not last
The least among the few

Generations will come and go
Like ashes in the breeze
None of us will have anything to show
Far less anyone to please

Lots of what I feel and know
Cannot be expressed in words
It's like a concert without a show
Or chirping without any birds

Can you imagine the end of existence?
Well I have already been there
And no amount of human persistence
Will change the circle into a square

PASSING BY

Many dawns
Will raise their head
And smile upon the land
Many relics
Of the many dead
Will wash up on the sand

Many moons
Will show their face
Many times a year
Many stars
Will fill their space
Long after we're not here

Many suns
Will disappear
And seek out other places
Many storms
Will spread their fear
Across all future faces

Many clouds
Will bring the rains
And the colours of the sky
Many rivers
Will flood the plains
While we pass on by

PUZZLING

I found a jigsaw piece
But the puzzle was missing
I found an empty box
It was full of intrigue
But no puzzle

I found a long lost story
It was full of mystery
I found so many clues
But still no puzzle
I found many ideas
And toyed with all of them
I found a problem lying around
And came up with a solution
But no puzzle

I found many obstacles
And tried to work them out
I found a list of answers
And tried to find the questions
But still no puzzle

RAW BLUES

Rhythms deep in my shoes
Nothing left for the imagination
Nothing left to choose

So what if you don't feel so good
The rhythm won't ever change
And you'll never be understood

If you're lucky enough to spell
Then the only way to heaven
Is through the path to hell

The rhythm that brings you satisfaction
Is deep within your soul
Waiting for the call of "action"

Sometimes when the brain is numb
The only beat you can hear
Is your own sole drum

When your rhythm becomes out of synch
Turn the bass right up
And pour yourself a drink

REACHING OUT

Reaching out
Conquering doubt
Offering a helping hand
Watching destiny
Sharing empathy
Helping to understand

Reaching out
To the silent shout
Listening from within
Being self-aware
Of one's own fear
Helping someone to begin

Reaching out
To find out about
To help and offer respect
Everyone needs
Some good deeds
Helping to re-connect

You have a right not to like this book
Under the rights of self-righteousness
You have a conscious objective to object
To the self consciousness of this book

REALITY

Shed a little light
On a certain matter
Cast a net
On what you can't see
Then turn away
From all the chatter
It's all just reality

Have a little cry
On somebody's shoulder
Throw down a line
Set someone free
Then turn away
Before you get older
It's all just reality
Make a little love
Spread a little kindness
Drop your anchor
Remove the complexity
Then turn away
From all the blindness
It's all just reality

RESTLESS THOUGHTS

In restless thoughts
I'm made aware
Of two-headed coins
That don't play fair

In senseless dreams
I'm shown the light
Of double standards
Made of fright

In twisted views
I have a path
Whichever way I take
It's all a laugh

In painted words
I'm shown the reason
Why so called friends
Are full of treason

You may feel shielded
Within your little bubble
But don't dare sneeze
Or you'll be in trouble

RUNNING AWAY

I tried running away from myself
But I didn't get very far
I tried overtaking my shadow
And almost got hit by a car

Even though I went to school
It didn't stop me from being a fool
It shows I haven't learnt very much
I'm older now but still out of touch

I tried running away from myself
Trying to avoid my destiny
I tried running into the woods
But ran straight into a tree

Even though I don't need advice
It doesn't mean I'm without a vice
Like a jungle made only of concrete
I'm still out of touch with my feet

I tried running away from myself
In a kind of self denial
But I ended up back in my cell
Like a man that's awaiting trial

SHALLOW INTAKE

With a shallow intake of breath
I leave my ego aside
But my legs are suddenly heavy
It's getting difficult to decide

Is there a deep-seated reason
Why I should feel the need to sleep?
Although I'm very much awake
I feel it's something deep

Maybe I'm looking for answers
That no one can ever find
Maybe I'm trying too hard to reach
A deep-seated shallow mind

I feel the need to become
What I don't really wish to do
I feel I need to address
What I know is simply untrue

With a shallow intake of awareness
I must detach each heavyweight
When it comes down to moving forward
My mind must re-evaluate

SIPPING COLD COKE

Here I am sitting on the edge of my bed in the early hours sipping cold
Coke in the dark
The only sound is the dawn chorus which is very pleasant as I sit in the
Dark sipping cold Coke
The cold coke quenches the indulgence of the previous hours as I sit in
The dark peacefully listening to the birds and sipping cold Coke
Absorbing the silence of the early hours I feel one step ahead of
Everyone
The only sound is the sipping of cold Coke and the occasional burp
Followed by the birds also absorbing the peace and one step ahead of
Everyone in the dark
How nice it would be to be able to recreate such an atmosphere but there
Would be no dark or silence or birds waking up
Guess I'll have to wait for another early morning

It's not a good sign to realise you're not ready
But it's not a bad sign to realise you're not

The problem created by making a mistake
Is not learning from the mistake
It's very easy to listen
But very hard to follow
Even though things may not work out
It does not mean it was not a good idea

The force between good and evil
Stretches the imagination
We're all stretched from birth to death
That's a big stretch in a short amount of time

SLOW MOTION

I see things in slow motion now
Rather than speeded up
What used to be a tumbler
Is now in a cup

What used to be extended egos
Are now cut down to size
I see words differently now
Especially the lies

I feel things in slow motion now
Especially the heartaches
What used to be taken for granted
Are no longer mistakes

What used to be accepted views
Are now carefully dissected
I feel a change in the air
I've been resurrected

I see people in slow motion now
I see them as they really are
What used to be so very close
Is now very far

SOMETHING

Something always happens
To put a spanner in the works
Something always appears
With its annoying little quirks

Something always surfaces
To make you feel unsure
Something you can't have
Is what you want even more

Something always speaks
To make you listen, turn and look
Something always moves
Like the words in an open book
Something always listens
To your D.N.A's ancient history
Something you can't have
Is what becomes a mystery

Something always amuses
The man with a straight face
Something always fills
The vacuum inside the space

SUDDEN DOWNPOUR (4.00 a.m.)

My friend the rain came calling
As all true friends do
It sounded as if in a hurry
I think it was just passing through
There was no fair warning
Or even a subtle creep
It shattered a complete silence
From a deepened comatose sleep
Suddenly my awakened attention
Was firmly in the now
There was no questioning of why
Or even a thought of how
It did not stay very long
But it made its presence known
There was a certain type of companionship
Even though I was alone
It left an air of calmness
Even though it was in a hurry
It took away my need to think
And even my need to worry

Never do anything
To make yourself look good
We all have our limitations
That have to be understood

Never step over your line
To become part of the race
Or you'll end up on your back
With egg over your face

Never become who you are not
To climb up a slippery pole
Or you'll become like so many
A square peg in a round hole

SUFFERING

Suffering rises
From desires
The burning
Of many fires

The fear of release
The price of peace
The need to aspire
The wheel of desire

Suffering breeds
From desires
The hidden tongues
Of many liars

The sound of sight
The noise of fright
The passing friend
The inevitable end

Suffering lives
From desires
God's will
Never tires

The dying herds
The Buddhist words
The life of death
The final breath

SUPER POWERS

Allegations
Have brought down nations
The thick black stuff
Is more than enough
To start the confrontations

The invisible force
Has come yet again
Through the portal
From another plain

Dimensions
Have caused surprises
Super powers delegate
A premeditated state
And cancelled many pensions

The dark force
Can blind your eyes
It's camouflage
It's hell of a disguise

Delegation
Is an art of persuasion
The game of chess
Becomes a mess
When the next move is invasion

THE HEART

Go where your heart
Says you must go
Go where the hurt
Doesn't show

If you cannot find
The answers in your mind
Look inside your heart
That's the place to start

Stay close to your heart
Rather than your mind
It's where the answers you seek
You will always find

Go where your heart
Says you must go
Go where intelligence
Doesn't know

THE ROOM NEXT DOOR

That which makes you thrive
The spark that keeps you alive
It has nothing to do with a choice
It's an engine
Formed by a voice

In your own personal drama
You have much to say
But it was all written for you
Like a script for a play

Different photographs
From different ages
Different stories
On different pages
Seeing the world
From a different view
What was old
Now seems new
Far away boundaries
Can be very near
Camouflaged views
Can turn to despair
That heartbeat
In your head
Is the constant riff
Until you're dead
The voices of your mum and dad
IS the D.N.A. of happy and sad
Who is at the controls of your plane
Who have you allowed inside your brain?

The past may seem so far away
And the future has nothing to say
But one thing is for sure
It's all in the room next door

THROUGH THE FIRE

Changing seasons
Have changed me
I've been through the fire
And felt the heat
I've been past the finishing line
And still felt defeat

Burnt out choices
And smouldering schemes
Smoked-filled voices
And charred dreams

Changing ideas
Have changed me
I've been through the fire
To the other side
I've been given promises
And still felt denied

Burt out desires
And smouldering delusions
Smoke-filled eyes
And denied illusions

TWO SUGARS

I like two sugars
In my tea
The bitterness of life
Does not appeal to me

The clock on the wall
Spells out destiny
I like two sugars
In my tea

When Winter steals
The leaves from the tree
It's then I love
Two sugars in my tea

I like two sugars
In my tea
Especially when rain clouds
Form a complexity

When doom and gloom
Comes through the TV
It's then I love
Two sugars in my tea

The clock on the wall
Spells out eternity
I like two sugars
In my tea

I like two sugars
In my tea
When I'm handcuffed
And unable to be free

WAITING

Waiting for something to happen
Waiting fort something to begin
Waiting for a thunderclap
Or even a bird to sing

Love is stranger than fiction
Day can be darker than night
Truth can be totally blind
But also full of sight
Waiting for a knock on the door
Waiting for the morning post
Waiting for lightning to strike
Or even a friendly ghost

Time is of the essence
In a long drawn-out day
Waiting for something to happen
Is only a phone call away

A NEED

We all need to sleep sometimes
We all need to weep sometimes
We all need a hand to hold
We all need to feel a little hold

We all need to hate sometimes
We all need to wait sometimes
We all need a reason to die
We all need to feel to try

We all need to respect sometimes
We all need to suspect sometimes
We all need a vision to see
We all need to feel a little free

We all need innuendoes sometimes
We all need to clean windows sometimes
We all need a God to follow
We all need to feel a need to swallow

We all need rejection sometimes
We all need dejection sometimes
We all need a need to shove
We all need to feel a little love

ALONE

You may have planted your acorns
And your trees are fully grown
But whatever you wish to accomplish
You just can't do it alone

Some days you might float above
Others you sink like a stone
But even though you're able to cope
You just can't do it alone

You may hold onto your morals
Like a dog holds onto a bone
But just like pride before a fall
You just can't do it alone

Some day full of praise
Others you just want to moan
The tide goes out, the tide comes in
You just can't do it alone

You may be the perfect model
Even though your children have flown
And though your duty is now over
You just can't do it alone

APPRECIATION AND UNDERSTANDING

If you don't hear noise
How can you appreciate the quiet?
If you never hurry
How can you appreciate being slow?
If you don't run
How can you appreciate walking?
If you don't compete
How can you appreciate losing?

Look for the calm
Inside the riot
Look for the warmth
Inside the cold
Look for the silence
Inside the talking
Look for the meaning
Inside the myth

DON'T PULL YOUR MASK OVER MY EYES

When the mask
You hide behind shatters
It's only then you find out
Who you really are
It's no good convincing me
That you were not
It's no good convincing me
That you are
For the person you were
Is the same person
Behind the mask…

BUBBLE

I want to be myself
In my own bubble
I don't want to incur
Your criticism and trouble

I want to write a book
In my own bubble
I don't want to shave
I want to feel my stubble

I want to think for myself
In my own bubble
I don't want to become
Someone else's double

I want to make mistakes
In my own bubble
Rather than become a brick
Lying in the rubble

BURDEN

I have released the burden
Of the arrows of bad feeling
That aimed directly at me
I have given away the burden
To the blind perpetrators
In the hope they will see me

I have carried the burden
Above and beyond any call of duty
In a kind of guilt complexity
I was forced to take this burden
As a lesson to be learnt
In a prison of necessity

The art of carrying a burden
Goes back to the beginning of time
It is an act of humility
The burden is a beast
It's a creature of habit
And continuous diversity

CALM

It calms me down
But opens me up
It's what is left
At the bottom of the cup

The lightning roars
The thunder strikes
Everything becomes
Likes and dislikes

The sweetness of life
Becomes very bitter
Reality becomes
What used to be glitter

The naked light of truth
Eventually strips
It's only when you're thinking
That reality grips

To be surrounded
When there's nobody there
Is a long journey
Without a spare

The more you learn
The less you know
And in the end
There's nothing to show

CAUGHT

I got caught up in the fishing net
While everyone else got away
I had sand in my shoes
And salt in my eyes
And not very much to say

I got caught up in the rubble
While everyone else crawled out
I had dust in my hair
And aches in my bones
And not very much to doubt

I got caught up in Russian roulette
While everyone else played chess
I had no choices
And no friends left
And not much else but stress

I got caught up in a breakdown
While everyone else played sane
I had blinded vision
And a misguided tongue
And nothing at all but pain

COMFORT ZONE

I like the dark
It suits me well
It's a comfort zone
In which I can dwell

I like the mist
It has no end
It's a comfort zone
Where I have a friend

I like the silence
It holds me close
It's a comfort zone
Like an overdose

I like the truth
It's full of tears
It's a comfort zone
Where no one dares

I like the unknown
It's full of schemes
It's a comfort zone
Of restless dreams

CONCEPT

Concepts go full circle
From the centre out
When the internal rumours start
And the sane begin to crumble
These are the signs of the times
When love is no longer happy
And tries to postpone the inevitable
Before the chemistry dries up
Shoved into a corner of your life
Made to grasp at invisible straws
Like an old English custom repeating itself
In a continuous monotonous circle
Picking yourself up from the train lines
And shocking everyone around you
The tight knot of frustration hurts
When you have to carry it around
It says so much about so little
In such a short period of time
Sleep walking through progress is lethal
Not sailing close but through the wind
Painting on emotions behind a visible mask
What you become is just an end product
Leaving you to finish the Grand design
Without human effort there is nothing
Only grasping in the darkness for a concept

IT'S ALL 3D

The man with the multi-coloured clothes
Has nothing important to say
But he says it well
It's amazing how trivia
Can become important
To someone caught up in a spell
He makes you feel someone
In a pretty mundane way
He takes you on a fantasy trip
In a world of make believe
Where repetition is very important
Even though you're losing your grip
In his psychedelic world of colour
He's become a total attachment
Infiltrating your quiet mind
He is a character of the street
A hallucination of human form
That becomes so easy to find
He has a statement to make
About the uncanny aspects of life
But no one can follow the thread
It's a no-win situation without an end
It's a dog that chases its tale
In a multi-coloured world inside his head

THE ONLY WAY
TO FIND AN ANSWER
IS NOT TO LOOK FOR IT

IF YOU HAVE TO THINK ABOUT IT
THEN YOU ALREADY KNOW THE ANSWER

NEVER, NEVER MAKE DECISIONS
WHEN INTOXICATED

IT

Insecure like sour grapes
Stubborn pride following from grace
Cutting off it's own nose
To spite its double face

Hamming up a childish act
Every day is a red herring day
Not just leading you up the path
But leading you astray

Always jumping every gun
Casting shadows like aspirations
Broken eggs in every basket
A figment of imaginations
Forever playing with mind games
Ideas now long in the tooth
Sentences that are full of innuendoes
Economic with the truth

Doing everything unto others
Watching lying dogs sleep
Lying through gold teeth that glitter
Counting chickens just like sheep

INTERLUDE

I just want to sit
In the warming sun
I just want to feel
Like having fun

I don't want to think
About the past
I just want this moment
To last

I just want to sit
In the warming glow
I just want to drift
I don't want to know

I don't want to speak
Or even memorise
I don't want to a lecture
Or surprise

I don't want to listen
To what is untrue
I just want to be
And not to do

IN THE DARK

In the dark
Truth is the same as lies
Nothing as it implies

The dumb become the wise
In the dark

In the dark
Satisfaction can be guaranteed
You don't have to be cut to bleed
Nothing you want can be all you need
In the dark

In the dark
Failures can be a token
Hearts can easily be broken
Dangerous words become unspoken
In the dark

IDEAS

Ideas are dangerous
Be careful how you tread
Think very carefully
Look inside your head
The delicate mechanics
That make up the machine
Can make you feel
What cannot be seen
Ideas are traps
Waiting to be sprung
They are invisible ropes
To get you hung
Ideas are dangerous
Be careful what you say
Take time out
To plan your day

When you follow ASSUMPTION
To become LAW
You create your own
JUDGE JURY AND EXECUTIONER

Follow your Heart
Instead of your brain
If they tell you to go to France
Then go to Spain

POPULARITY BREEDS RABBITS

I ONCE

I once was a loose cannon
With symbolic gesturing fingers
Full of experienced induced states
Whose memory sometimes lingers

I once had gallows humour
And was very highly strung
Full of myself and no one else
Which almost got me hung

I once had an acid tongue
And could not tread carefully
And those who came to lunch
No longer came to tea

I once had blinkered vision
And laughed at everyone's fear
But hindsight was ahead of me
And stripped my ego bare

I once had no fear of God
Full of brass and just as bold
The house that once said bought
Has now gone up as sold

I

I am I
The I that does
And the I that does not
But watches the I that does
I criticises I
The I that watches
Imprisons the I that does
The I that acts
Is a limited I
A prisoner of its own I
It becomes a split I
A prisoner I
A judge I
A surrendering I
A false I
A new I
A spiteful I
A lost I
A Jekyll and Hyde I
A Rasta I and I
I am
Therefore I exist I
But the I
That divides in two
Is the only I
In the equation
It's an I
That surrounds itself
With itself
It's a lonely I
And all in the blink of an eye

HAPPY CHILD

It's nice to hear a child
That's happy and free
Full of contentment love and glee

It's nice to hear a child
Laughing with its dad
No hint of aggression,
fear or being sad

It's nice to hear a child
Happy with its mum
High as a kite, bouncy and never glum
It's nice to hear a child
Full of self-esteem
Not suppressed or depressed
but part of a team

It's nice to hear a child
Not bitter but very sweet
Not bullied or tormented,
just skipping on its feet

EXPRESSION

I can feel an expression coming on
But it's not on my face
It must be somewhere hidden
In a secluded place

It walks with shoulders back
And feels six foot high
It walks without any fear
And seems to touch the sky

I can feel an expression coming on
But it's not on my face
It must be somewhere drifting
In and out of space

It walks with a swagger
And feels like a top dog
It speaks with the confidence
Of falling off a log

I can feel an expression coming on
But it's not in my reflection
It must be somewhere in the mirror
Looking for a direction

VENEMOUS SNIPERS
NOT ONLY HIDE IN THE GRASS
AND NOT ALL VIPERS
ARE BEHIND A GLASS

DOUBLE STANDARDS

If you have no love
Then you have no tears
The obvious becomes
A world of fears

The constant dripping
That wears the stone
Makes all those surrounded
Still feel alone

The outstretched arms
That want to reach you

May not be the ones
That need to teach you

And in the darkness
Comes the light
Only seen by a few
With an inner sight

The silent drummer
Is within us all
And those who are deaf
Will most certainly fall

Visions we see
Are all blind
If the true path
We cannot find

Sometimes insincerity
Is but a joke
When surrounded by
Insincere smoke

So judge yourself
Like you judge me
Like a pardoned prisoner
Who's never free

When you look in the mirror
It's not what you see
It's the reflection
That wants to be free

When writing feelings
Becomes a fright
It's only the difference
Between day and night

When you listen to something
Which is pre-occupied
Then you must turn away
And become dissatisfied

When the song is over
And you open the door
Don't be depressed because
There is no floor

The grip of vengeance
Can never be free
Unless you release your conscience
From the prison you can see

When your Birthday cake
Reminds you of yesterday
Blow out the candles
And turn yourself away

How many lies
Can you misunderstand
Before the penny drops
In no man's land?

One false step
Becomes a crime
The slippery slope
Through a different time

From the jealous minds
That taunt the night
Come hidden eyes
Without any sight

And when it's time
For you to swear
You'll find yourself
Hard to compare

So many visions
In so many a sound
A world full of revolutions
Like a merry-go-round

Life is a cocktail
Laced with trouble
Each and every standard
Is not single but double

DEEPEST FEELINGS

The deepest feelings are the hardest ones to show, the only way they
Reach the surface is when two souls become one
Life is short as time slips through our fingers but with love by our side we
Can make time stand still

Love is an art form, sharing, caring, understanding, forgiving, loving
Invisible forces can blind true feelings when negative feelings enter our
Lives, the one we love is the first to be hurt but deep-seated roots will
Always stay firmly anchored, no matter how stormy it may be
In the search for happiness, there are many ports in a storm, through
All life's constant journeys rough and smooth, no matter how many
miles,
You always know when you've finally arrived.
True commitment is very hard to find but a soul full of pride can conquer
Any relationship, it is the ray of sun that shines through the dark clouds
True love is a never-ending stream, it flows forever, no matter what
Obstacles, it is eternal

WHAT IS DONE

What is done
You can lock the door
Pack your bag
Or even run
You can disconnect the phone
Pull the curtains
Cover your eyes
And think alone
What is done is done

If you don't try to
Find yourself sometimes
You'll most certainly
End up losing yourself
Completely

DEEP

What people think
Can be hard to tell
Like long lost secrets
In an ancient well

Who knows what lies
Deep within
Sleeping in time
Waiting to begin?

Thoughts become worn
Like a rusty gate
No longer new
And hard to penetrate

Words become choked
Like flowers by weeds
Expression dries up
When silence bleeds

Behind stone walls
Many a whisper echoes
Thoughts can hide deep
Where no one goes

CONSEQUENCE

When a subtle breeze
Is on the tease
Listen to the chime
And the words that rhyme
For it's the total surprise
That makes you wise
If you look inside
Where fearful people hide
You'll feel the shock
Of the submissive block
You don't need eyes to see
The hate in your society
You don't need to touch to feel
Or even rob yourself to steal
When a subtle stare
Makes you disappear
Listen to the voice
And the wisdom of choice
For being on the brink
Can make you sink
If love is a vice
In a game of dice
You'll always walk alone
And be on your own
You don't need roads to walk
Or listen to the clever talk
You don't need experience to think
Or two eyes to make you blink
If you sit on both sides of the fence
Then be prepared to take the consequence

YES

No matter what the issues
Whether more or less
Whatever the answer
Let it be a yes

Despite your views
And despite how you dress
Stand firm and believe
The answer is yes

No matter what the problems
Though your life's a stress
Whatever the answer
Let it be a yes

Despite the hatred
And tormented mess
Stand firm and believe
The answer is yes

No matter the surroundings
Or change of address
Whatever the turmoil
Let it be a yes

WHO AM I TODAY?

Who am I today
As the dawn chorus clears its throat?
Will I see past the veil
Or stare at the ceiling and gloat?

Who am I today
As the sunlight seeps through the curtain?
Will I see past the mist
That makes the future uncertain?

Who am I today
As the drum in the distance echoes?
Will I see past the muffled sound
That infiltrates and grows?
Who am I today
As the sunset paints its final touch?

Will I see past the hurdles?
I doubt it very much

WHAT AM I?

Live by myself
But I'm not alone
Can change my thought
By change of tone
I'm happy being in
I'm happy being out
The silence you hear
Is really a shout!

I have my own space
And a blank cheque
I'm the missing card
In a shuffled deck
Sometimes I'm in front
Sometimes I'm behind
I have an intuition
But can be blind

I enjoy talking
And sometimes not
I can run cold
And very hot
I can be patient
I can jump the gun
I can be psychotic
And even fun

I hate isolation
But like my space
I can change my feelings
By change of place
I am honest
But can deny
I am a riddle

What am I?

WATCHING

Watching jealous feelings
In conflict
Watching confused minds
Lose direction
It's like being on valium
In the sunshine
Watching misunderstandings
Lose control
Watching the nightmares
In the daytime
It's like a sacrifice
Without any boundaries
Watching the illusions
Slowly unfold
Watching cold hearts
Unable to beat
It's like unturned stones
Devoid of deceit
Watching separate worlds
Pass each other
Watching the temptations
On their mission
It's like beating a heart
Without any blood

WALK-IN-SPIRIT

Someone walked in
As I walked out
I'm now someone else
There is now doubt

Someone walked in
To set me free
And from the darkness
I now can see

Someone walked in
To take my place
I'm no longer the same
Despite my face

Someone walked in
To take my name
I'm now returned
From whence I came
Someone walked in
To release the pain
To follow my path
And take the strain

URGENCY

There's a certain sense of urgency
That courses through my veins
It's the thunder and lightning
That precedes the coming rains

There's a rush of sudden urgency
As I drop into enemy terrain
A pulsating feeling of anxiety
That somehow I'll miss the train

There's a panic attack of urgency
Not to become my age
This constant fear of passing time
And no writing on the page

There's a cash flow of urgency
That some are forced to endure
It's okay if you're rich
But not much fun if you're poor

There's a flood of certain urgency
That fills me with dread
It's fiction that becomes the fact
The fact that you'll soon be dead

TRAPPED

Someone has messed up the computer
The motherboard is under threat
The decision that is made today
Could become tomorrow's regret

Thank you for the invite
It's truly a very nice house
The ceiling is so very high
I feel like a tiny mouse,
Thank you for showing me around
I like the polished floor
Just as a matter of interest
Have you got a back door?

Thank you for your hospitality
And the conversational flow
If the walls happen to close in
Have you got a side window?
If you have any sudden plans
I would appreciate it if you say
Don't hold back coming forward
I don't want to out-welcome my stay

I'm afraid I must anxiously warn you
Relaxation for me is handicapped
What you call unconditional freedom
To me is an animal trapped

TOO MANY SHOES

Too many shoes
To confuse the eyes
Too many sounds
And tissues of lies

Too many voices
And choices to make
Too many directions
And tablets to take

Too many views
And clues to find
Too many suggestions
In an overloaded mind

Too many shoes
To choose a solution
Too many words
And no resolution

THER IS NO SUCH THING AS WORRY
IT'S ALL IN THE MIND
CONTROL THE MIND
AND YOU CONTROL WORRY

THE WALK

I walked down the road
Whistling a tune
It must have been
Just before noon
I walked very slowly
It felt great
I then lost touch of time
Even though I was late

I walked a path
I never walked before
I found many keys
To many a door
I stopped many times
Inside my head
To meet the me
I thought was dead

I walked the path of Karma
Without having to fret
There was something familiar
About everyone I met
The clouds changed form
Like the thoughts in my brain
It was like travelling
On a very slow train

I walked down the road
Humming a tune
The day was perfect
Like a full moon
I glided without thinking
And hoping it would last
My heart was at peace
And no longer beating fast

THE VILLAGE GREEN

Oh beautiful sunshine
We've been waiting for you to arrive
Our team's losing wickets
I doubt we can survive
It's nice to see your smiling face
And your atmosphere serene
Could you please spread yourself
Across the village green
There's a lovely smell of linseed oil
Of well worn gloves and pads
Could you stretch yourself a little
And help our failing lads
It's been a while since any runs
There's a stillness across the lawn
The odd four or six would be quite handy
Before the stumps are drawn
Please help our boys to whack the ball
Give the fielders something to chase
I think they've had too much of the cider
And are beginning to feel the pace
The early rain has dampened spirits
We need your helping hand
We need a jolly hefty six
Straight into the members' stand
The score board's gone to sleep I fear
The run rate's a little fraught
Because of the moisture and slippery surface
Our edges are being caught
We need some warming influence
Like six over the proverbial tree
The older legs are feeling the strain
And hoping it's time for tea
The cider's cold but the sun is warm
Which helps on a sticky wicket
Ass the sun goes down across the green
It simply has to be cricket

THE TAP IS DRIPPING

The tap is dripping today
There's a slight chill in the air
I'm snug in my bed
Devoid of any fear

It's here and now
Not then and there
We make the choice
Of freedom or despair

It's what we are
Not what we become
It's difficult for many
And harder for some

It's all about today
Not future satisfaction
It's like lusting for tomorrow
And hoping for gratification

The tap is definitely dripping
There's a breeze through the curtain
I may be snug in my bed
But nothing is ever certain

At that particular moment in time
When everything is at its pinnacle
I make the mistake of thinking
And sincerity slips into cynical

The headlights hit me square on
And catches me in disguise
The meaning of why I am
Is lost in both my eyes

THE HOUNDS

The hounds are at my door
Nostrils flared and ivory fangs
And the feelings I'm feeling inside
Is definitely not hunger pangs

The hounds with eyes of steel
Are waiting to tear me apart
And the feelings I'm feeling inside
Are not for the faint of heart

The hounds have found where I live
And are itching to get me out
And the feelings I'm feeling inside
Are leaving me without any doubt
The hounds are howling for blood
And they all look like you and I
And the feelings I'm feeling inside
Is something I cannot deny

WORRY AND HURRY
IS A TASTELESS CURRY

WHEN YOU ACCEPT THE ROLE AS
AN INNOCENT BYSTANDER IN LIFE
THE BURDEN OF LIFE BECOMES LESS HEAVY

ADVICE IS THE EASIEST THING TO GIVE
AND THE HARDEST THING TO TAKE

THE BEAT OF A THE DRUM

Golly sits and smiles
Benjamin Bear sits on his chair
The cross-legged Indian smokes his pipe
And the Wolf on the wall shows no fear
There is no such thing as freedom
You are what you will become
The loss of control is quite normal
It is the missing beat of the drum
I've been branded as a liar
I've been branded as a square
I've had many backs turned against me
And forced to live a life of fear
Why say you love me
To make me feel insecure?
Why can't you face who you are
And not make me feel unsure?
No one has a minute to spare
But everyone has a price
And all I've ever been to anyone
In the roll of the dice
What means a lot to other people
Means nothing at all to me
I died many centuries ago
But I've never been allowed to be free
What is black is black
What is blue is blue
But nothing can erase
The truth behind what's true

STONEWORK

The knowledge of being in command
Is the stonework of your ego
But when cracks appear and uncertainty seeps in
The foundations can crumble below

Fortunate circumstances create no illusions
And are the cornerstone of your pride
But when reality smashes the stonework
There is nowhere you can hide

The stonework is laid from the cot
The last safe comfort zone
Hurtful foundations become like a plague
It's inevitability you cannot postpone

Be conscious of your awareness
And be aware of who you are
For the stonework of your world
Can become extremely bizarre

STONED WITHOUT DOPE

What makes you tick?
Is it a clock?
What keeps you fastened?
Is it a lock?

Is the shadow in the corner
Really Jack Horner?
Are all animals with a fleece
Unable to give Mary any peace?

What turns a biscuit
Into a crumb?
Why are signs
Important to the dumb?

Are the staring eyes that gloat
Really an owl and a cat in a boat?
Does leadership come at a price?
Did the pied piper hate all mice?

What is the switch
That lights up hell?
Is it a witch
Casting a spell?

What was the real fear
That caused Miss Muffet's scare?
Does every problem have an enigma
Like Humpty Dumpty and his stigma?

So what is left but a candid view
The fact I have to say hello to you
I feel I can just about cope
Being stoned without any dope

SPIRITUAL LAWS

Today I shall judge nothing and no one
Everything is as it should
Stay grounded in the wisdom of uncertainty
Step into the field of all possibilities
We are pure consciousness and awareness
End the struggle and go with the flow
Be surrounded by silence and inner peace
Seek the stillness that lies within
Remain in the state of self-referral, the world of
The self, the true being, be in control and not
Others
Intention and desire must be grounded in the
Detached freedom of the present
Accept things as they are
Accept responsibility for your own actions and
Feelings
Resist defending points of view
Avoid resisting what is
The past is history, the future is a mystery and the
Present is all there is
I am that, you are that, all this is that and that's
All there is

SOMETHING

Something planned long ago
Inside my head has been planted
What it is I do not know
That luxury has not been granted

Something has been growing
Like a concern deep inside
Like understanding without really knowing
Waiting for someone to decide

Something was set in motion
Something neither wrong nor right
Like the sunset on the ocean
And the passing ships in the night

Something I cannot see
Reminds me I'm not in control
Someone is standing beside me
And controlling my very soul

SMALL SACRIFICE

This stabbing feeling that sacrifice brings
A monotonous tone that constantly sings
A winning solution that has no prize
Words of iron that vaporise
Someone has chosen your sacrifice
To walk forever on a field of ice
Do you have it or does it have you?
Restrained eyes are forced to view
It takes the sound of falling rain
To release the grip and ease the pain
What use to be just once or twice
Is now acres on the horizon of sacrifice

Planning ahead of yourself
Thinking ahead of yourself
Racing ahead of yourself
Happy being ahead of yourself
It's all on your mobile text
But it is better to be late in this world
Than early in the next

See things as they are
And not how you want them to be
A bird is for the tree
And a fish for the sea
You are you
And I am me

SHARK

Caught in the shallow end
Trapped within a net
Alone without a friend
And smell of fear in the sweat

This is not make believe
Only a trapped agility
Being different can deceive
The best of any ability

The strong and silent lurking beneath
Is fear looking for the open sea
Frustration trapped in clenched teeth
A predator desperate to be free

Forever prone to the snap decision
Caught in a web of intrigue
The perfect machine of precision
A thrashing mind of fatigue

There's something mystical, strange but weak
Trapped within a net
It says a lot but cannot speak
And it's definitely not a pet

RUSTY LOCKS AND CHAINS

We lock ourselves out
We lock ourselves in
We like to give up
Before we begin

Rusty locks and chains
Seal our hearts away
Keeping us from coming out to play

We want to be quiet
We want to shout
We're free to speak
But locked in doubt
Rusty locks and chains
Seal our minds away
Keeping our own Wolves at bay

We hate the day
We hate the night
We all like to give up
Before the fight

Rusty locks and chains
Seal our fates away
Keeping us bound for another day

ROAD OF NO RETURN

Unforgiving thoughts
Coupled with guilt
And frustration
Is a long forgotten
Deserted station

Pride based
On eccentric ego
And aimless suspicions
Is a bold army
Sent on futile missions

Where tracks
Lead nowhere
And bridges never burn
Is where the signs says
The road of no return

SQUEAKY CLEAN

Are you squeaky clean
When you climb upon your stage?
Are you the perfect scene
From behind your painted rage?

Are you squeaky clean
When you speak with an open mind?
Are you the perfect screen
For your image to hide behind?

Are you squeaky clean
Especially behind your ears?
Are you the perfect machine
With all your fancy gears?

RIGHT TIME RIGHT PLACE

What have you brought
From the passing years?
Was it plenty of laughter?
Was it plenty of tears?

Was it a breakfast of dope
That gave you hope?
Was it the smiling faces
Or the right time and right places?

Was it the people that you've met
That made you feel no regret?
Was it the lack of confinement in open spaces
Or the right time and the right places?

Was it the drought of immortality
That led to eventuality?
Was it the people stacked full of aces
Or the right time and the right places?

What have you brought
From the setting sun?
Was it segments of sorrow
Or was it segments of fun?

POETIC

I'm a poetic tailor
I'm a pied piper with his flute
Give me your ideas
And I'll make you a suit

I'm a poetic sailor
I'm an avid mountaineer
Give me your request
And I'll bring you back a souvenir

I'm a poetic diver
I'm constantly looking for pleasure
Give me your wishes
And I'll bring you back a treasure

I'm a poetic spaceman
I'm a traveller of speed
Give me your vision
And I'll find you what you need

I'm a poetic philosopher
I'm a maker of schemes
Give me your soul
And I'll give you my dreams

PLASTERCINE PEOPLE

The changing face on gravestones
The changing of flesh to bones
The changing of yesterday's views
Shapes today and tomorrow's news

Plastercine people full of fear
Moulded into a complexity of despair
Plastercine people of different races
Moulded into a complexity of faces

The changing of static phases
The different meaning of different phrases
Like many emotions locked in a fridge
Only to become water under the bridge

Plastercine people full of lies
Moulded into a camouflage of disguise
Plastercine people of different ideas
Moulded into a camouflage of tears

The changing faces without ears
The changing of confidence to fears
The changing of silence to noise
Today's psychosis is tomorrow's toys

PERFECT

Such a perfect scene
Ripples in the stream
Peace in its motion
Echoing in the woods
Such a perfect sky
Splashed in paint
Perfection in colour
By an invisible artist

Such a perfect garden
With scents that ease
Welcoming butterflies
Gathering around
Such a perfect night
The moon and stars reign
Trees remain silent
The air is asleep

Such a perfect day
Sunshine warms the soul
Sleeping into the bones
Taking away the pain
Such a perfect wine
Slipping down with ease
Opening up visions
That flow through the veins

Such perfect music
Drowns the soul
Suddenly who you feel
Is who you are
Such a perfect end
Problems are dissolving
Feeling like someone else
Is such a boost

PASSING THOUGHT

Anyone can self-destruct
It has nothing to do with luck
You don't have to pay any toll
Anyone can lose control

We can create illusionary scenes
In our tightly fitting depressing genes
We all have or can eventually fail
And no warning lights will prevail

When decisions become a wild guess
People see it as a form of excess
When the weight you carry becomes a drag
It's just an insecure emotional bag

For the unfortunate there is no peace
Only suppressed demons screaming for release
And the feeling that's lost its direction
Is love looking for some kind of affection

SOMETIMES THE TRUTH
IS BETTER THAN
A PEACEFUL ANSWER
AND SOMETIMES A PEACEFUL ANSWER
IS BETTER THAN THE TRUTH

PACKED FULL

It's a complicated story
Packed full of glory
And lost causes
Ups and downs
Packed full of sounds
And full of pauses

Times and tides
Packed full of reflections
And much confusion
Friends and spies
Packed full of lies
And full of delusion

It's a complicated mess
Packed full of stress
And emotional hopping
Running miles
Packed with smiles
And all without stopping

Symptoms and allergies
Packed full of formalities
And much debate
Acts and solutions
Packed full of illusions
And much hate

OVERLOAD

The mental scars
Like bald tyres on cars
Is not what you deserve
When you have to swerve
Onto a different road
With a very heavy load
And very dodgy brakes
Making many mistakes
No one pays any heed
As you race by in top speed
Can't help the way you feel
Hanging on to the steering wheel
So much experience with dejection
As you lose complete direction
Trying to keep within the lines
Trying to recognise all the signs
But there's nothing in the Highway Code
To suggest how to deal with overload

ONE OF THOSE

I like to say
What I have to
And then leave
I'm not one of those
Long-winded preachers
Who feel they have to grieve

I like to look
At what I see
And tie it in a bow
I'm not one of those
Long gifted speakers
Who will tell you everything they know

I like to show
Whatever I feel
As quickly as can be
I'm not one of those
Long distance runners
Who take you through everything they see

I like to write
What stirs inside
And make it quite concise
I'm not one of those
Long dead poets
Who died not once but twice

OLD AGE

Where were you
When I was young
When I thought only
With a slippery tongue?

There was no old age
Only parents and relatives
Were supposed to be old
And only the young
Were supposed to be bold

Everlasting youth
Would be with me
Forever and ever
Or so I thought
When I thought I was clever

As time disappeared
Fear took hold
Just before thirty
Like a disease
Forty was something dirty

Time galloped
Leaving youth
Looking over its shoulder
Now for once
Youth felt older

Forty came
And forty went
Like a hurricane
Causing total devastation
And mental pain

Old age
How swift you were
And so unkind
What was so far ahead
Is now so far behind

MULTIPLE

Multiple changes in the weather
Multiple changes in moods
Multiple changes in finances
Multiple changes in foods

Everything has to be multiplied
It is futile to resist
Nothing of worth is simplified
Otherwise we can't exist

Multiple changes in the law
Multiple changes in schools
Multiple changes in correctness
Multiple changes in rules

Everything has to be multiplied
It's not fiction it is fact
Nothing of worth is singular
Or else they'll make it an act

Multiple changes in the government
Multiple changes in security
Multiple changes in friendship
Multiple changes in identity

Everything has to be multiplied
To save the future from flaws
Is it the sign of the times
Or are we cats without any claws?

MOVE FORWARD

The past has gone now
Let's not reminisce
Let's move forward
Beyond that elusive kiss

The time is right now
Let's not presume
Let's move forward
And begin to resume

The past has no future
Let's not stay there
Let's move forward
And strip ourselves bare
The time is here and now
Let's not forget
Let's move forward
Without any regret

The time has come now
Let's not be blurred
Let's speak of now
And make ourselves heard

MAGAZINE ARTICLE

I've been everywhere
I've done everything
I've had pineapple
And orange juice
But nothing can really compare
To being covered in chocolate mousse

I've seen many people
I've been to many places
I like driving, walking
Even staying at home
But nothing can really compare
To being covered in creamy foam

I've been married
I've been divorced
I've had many jobs, women
And many a car
But nothing can really compare
To the taste of a Mars Bar

LUV ETERNAL

May the sun shine strong
As you walk the path of glory
May the luv within your heart
Speak a true luv story

May your luv be eternal
And keep you from being apart
May you be not two but one
Within a single beating heart

May the pass inside be healed
And all the hypocrisy pass you by
May your spirit shine forever
Like a rainbow in the sky

May you always walk together
When you next hear the dove
May the Great Spirit embrace you
As you walk the path of luv

WHEN YOU SURRENDER

When you surrender
To the present
Life is a lot more
Bearable

Do what you feel
Not what is expected

I may be a fool
But I'm not your fool

LOSING THE PLOT

I think you're losing the plot
You seem to know everything but not a lot
You seem to wear more than you've got

Even though the writing's on the wall
Deaf ears don't hear the call
In your world there is no doubt
Closed doors keep people out

What sleeps within and cannot wake
Becomes that illogical mistake
Signs and directions become slurred
Reason and thinking becomes blurred

Concrete walls become a domain
Love and understanding becomes a pain
Those who are close become very far
And loneliness becomes who you are

I think you're losing the plot
You want to gallop but can't even trot
You want to know the truth but not what

LONELY TOWN

I'm just passing through
In this lonely town
Every time I smile
It's met by a frown
I must sacrifice myself
All over again
In order to cut through
Other people's pain

In the warm summer sun
Cold hearts pass me
I realise yet again
It's my destiny
Although I listen
There is no sound
Only fragile minds
On solid ground

I'm just passing through
This very lonely town
All I seek is simplicity
But I feel like a clown
I smile at people
They show me their tears
But I've already been there
For so many years

I EXIST

The conspiracy of silence
In the cupboards of families
Is death in small doses
Surrounded by supposes
And the skeletons of the past

There is no cold comfort
From the cultural protection
When reality becomes very stark
And the whispers in the dark
Become biologically dysfunctional

There is no request put in
For existence to be implanted
So speak to me, don't deny me
Respect me, don't deject me
I am, therefore, I exist

KIDS

We are like kids to a playground
Given our own free will
They skate over obstacles
While we climb uphill

The solutions we seek
Are not hard to find
Kids find the answers
While we stumble blind

When kids are upset
We don't see the reason
We wear the Crowns
And they are the treason

And when the past is forgotten
From January to December
Innocence becomes
How far back you remember

JUST DO IT

If you need to get away
From yourself for just a day
Then just do it
If it helps you to forget
Everything that you regret
Then just do it

For life moves very fast
Its shadow soon to cast
And the time it takes to think
Is lost in just a blink

If you feel like opening a door
To some place you've not been before
Then just do it
If self-esteem has gone astray
And you feel the need to pray
Then just do it

For life won't wait around
For your feet to touch the ground
And the time you thought would last
Will suddenly be the past

I'M FIFTY PLUS

Please mum don't make a fuss
I'm not five you know
I'm fifty plus

Hello Mum
Nice to hear from you again
What's that?
I'll catch a cold
If I stand out in the rain
I mustn't go out in the wind
In case I get hit by a tree
I'm fifty plus Mum
Not bloomin' three

What's that Mum
If I'm going out driving
Don't have a drink
It's a good thing you rang Mum
After fifty plus
I've forgotten how to think

I've been living as a man
For all these years
And not a wind-up toy
I'm a son who needs affection, yes
But not treated like a boy

Yes Mum
I've got it all in rhyme
Because you see it's all in my head
I heard it all the last time

AN EARTHQUAKE HAPPENED

An earthquake happened
They know how
But they don't know why
My mind shifted
They know how
But they don't know why.

A tsunami happened
They know how
But they don't know why
My mind was submerged
They know how
But they don't know why.

A tornado happened
They know how
But they don't know why
My mind was blown away
They know how
But they don't know why.

I DON'T KNOW WHAT CAUSES IT
But I know it's always there
IT'S NOT AT ALL UNREASONABLE
And it's not entirely fair.

Lightning Source UK Ltd.
Milton Keynes UK
174917UK00001B/22/P